EXPLORING
WITH PAINT

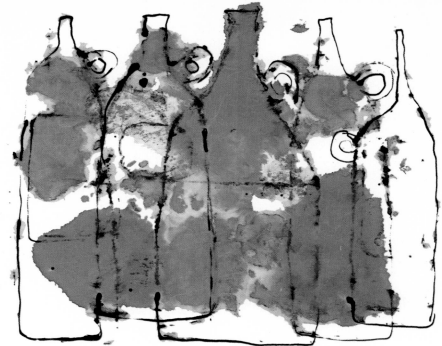

Stick painting

Roller painting

EXPLORING WITH PAINT

Henry Petterson and Ray Gerring

REINHOLD BOOK CORPORATION/NEW YORK

Acknowledgments

The authors wish to express deep appreciation to the following persons for their contributions to the development of this book:

Professor Boyer Gonzales, Director of the School of Art, University of Washington, Seattle, who offered initial assistance and stimulus.

Dr. Herbert Reas, Dean of the School of Education, Seattle University, who provided kind encouragement.

Miss Audrianna Allen, Elementary Assistant, Seattle Public Schools, who read the manuscript for clarity.

William Ransdell, commercial photographer, who handled the photographic requirements of the work with enthusiasm and efficiency.

Added thanks are due to the many colleagues and the pupils who, in addition to their paintings, offered criticism and helpful suggestions during the course of the development of this book.

Designed by Emilio Squeglio
Type set by Graphic Arts Typographers, Inc.
Printed by Halliday Lithograph Corporation
Bound by Publishers Book Bindery

Contents

Preface

Contained in this stimulating series of approaches to painting is more than technical aid. An analysis of the techniques presented reveals a healthy visual bias. As each medium of expression is explored one can discern the foundations upon which these lessons rest. The student and teacher are clearly guided to expend attention and energy on *visual qualities*— the exciting *textural effects* which can be created, *color variations, value changes* that build aesthetic interest, and *lines* full of variety and movement. Development of these visual concerns constitutes the core of art teaching. To free the child from a literal, verbal cocoon which tends to insulate his imagination and place his powers of perception into hibernation, the successful teacher must employ creative classroom pursuits based on basic art judgments. The elements of fine visual judgment are presented in strength through technical aids.

Without adequate technical information art instruction will be unsubstantial indeed, resulting in unnecessary student floundering. Sustained interest is maintained with demonstrations which spark the sense of adventure and experimentation. Guidance, direction, and motivation should precede and lead to student discovery. The teacher who is well prepared to teach technique supplies a valuable vehicle for exploration; he is better able to assist students in expanding creative boundaries.

Creativity and skill may grow simultaneously; they are certainly mutually supportive. Confidence for the timid starts with gaining control of a medium—a vital component upon which creativity rests. There is danger that instruction may stop at this point—with pure unadulterated "how-to-do-it." It is in the handling of this delicate matter that the strength of this volume lies. The authors give us generous indications of concern for creative teaching—an elusive factor which few books communicate.

The series of painting concepts contained here are viewed by the authors as "springboards for further exploration." The creative teacher will use them as intended: as door openers, to arouse imagination, and as useful interest builders. If he seeks a fine blend of helpful mechanics and of exploratory stimulation, this book is for him.

Dr. J. D. Stoops, Art Department
University of California at Los Angeles

Organizing for Painting

THE PURPOSE

The purpose of *Exploring with Paint* is twofold: to assist the classroom teacher and pupils in developing original methods of painting that are stimulating and imaginative, and to explore a wide range of painting processes in order to offer relief from some of the restrictions imposed by the limitations inherent in any one painting tool or method.

As an example, the brush has long been depended upon by pupils as their major painting tool. The brush is usually readily available in the classroom, but because there is an increased need to accommodate the wide variety of abilities and needs of these young painters, several different ways of using the brush are suggested along with other choices of painting tools such as the squeegee, sponge, and stick.

The technical proficiency required by any one tool in painting has developed in many pupils a feeling of *inadequacy*. This feeling is not justified when one considers the minor importance of tools as compared with the pupil's ideas and the possible imaginative visual experiences he may attain.

The imagination of the pupil should be considered his greatest asset. The ideas and suggestions presented should be thought of in terms of a need for an awareness of the mechanics involved in many varied methods of painting. The methods described are stepping stones to further means of expression in the field of painting.

Many of the methods included here have characteristics borrowed from other art forms and mediums; for example, the technique of printmaking contributes to the development of cardboard painting (p. 16).

One should not assume that the use of imaginative painting techniques alone will guarantee initial success for the pupil. Additional growth is needed in his understanding and development of the simple basics of composition before real confidence and continued good results can be achieved. *Exploring with Paint* takes the view that painting is an area of study in which constant change is normal, in which new ideas are always welcome and should flourish. It is hoped that the material provided will prove exciting and give needed knowledge of painting to classroom teachers.

In summary, the principal significance of this guide is *to offer inspiration* and to stimulate the pupils' interest in painting; *to provide information* covering a variety of painting materials, tools, and processes; *to motivate, challenge and encourage* the young painter to discover for himself many of the different ways to express his ideas through painting.

CLASSROOM PAINTING SPACE

Although many classrooms are not specifically designed for painting experiences and may present obstacles to the extensive kind of exploratory painting program desired, merely having very fine facilities does not always guarantee successful painting experiences for pupils.

Each classroom must be adapted to the individual teacher's painting needs. If desk tops are too small, then floors, tables, and counter tops should be used. If display space in the room is limited, then other places in the building may serve equally well. If water is not available, storage containers will need to be brought in. Each space is unique and needs to be analyzed to see what possibilities it offers and what plans can be made for adjustment and improvement, even though they may be modest.

There are several important general considerations for the teacher when making plans for the painting experience:

Storage and Care of Painting Materials

Cupboards, shelves, and cabinets that are available for storing painting materials must often be shared with other classroom needs. If the room is designed specifically for art, the problem of storage is not so great. Otherwise, specific storage areas must be designated in the classroom to house the tools and materials for painting. These areas should be accessible to pupils or at least to selected helpers who may assist the teacher in setting up the painting session and putting things away when it is over. Materials and tools require monitors for dispensing and collecting. This system works well, especially if the classroom area is somewhat cramped and simultaneous movement of large numbers of pupils needs to be curtailed. If the facilities are more ample, then another

A common shoe box or, in this case, a larger boot box provides pupils with their own painting tool storage.

approach can be used: A counter or table with all the necessary materials spread out should be provided so that pupils can serve themselves cafeteria style. Another way of handling materials is to provide each pupil with a shoe box or similar container in which to store most of the necessary painting tools. Each pupil is then responsible for the care of his equipment for the full year's work. This has the advantage of placing responsibility on each pupil rather than on the teacher or a monitor.

Work Areas

Since table or desk tops usually serve the pupils in many ways, it is important that these areas be kept reasonably clean. Newspapers are an effective means to protect these surfaces. After a painting session, the newspapers can be discarded, leaving the desks ready for the next activity. Other table coverings include sheet plastic and oil cloth, but they are not disposable and so present a storage problem, especially when wet or soiled.

If the classroom is equipped with movable tables, desks, and seats, it is easier to arrange for painting experiences. If desks are stationary, however, the floor is the most logical place for pupils to paint.

If the room is not equipped with a sink and drainboard, water can be brought in containers to the classroom, and waste or cleanup water can be discarded in the lavatory areas at the end of the painting session.

Storage of Paintings

No problem is more vexing than cleaning up after the painting session and storing the paintings to dry. Many paints, even water-soluble paints, normally quick to dry, may require thirty minutes or longer to dry completely. Thirty-six or more damp paintings cannot be neatly piled on top of each other. Neither can they be pinned to the bulletin board, since wet paint runs quite readily. Paintings must be left to dry flat, each in an individual place.

Table tops which must be protected for other activities can be covered with newspapers.

If classroom tables and desks are difficult to use, the floor provides an excellent place to paint (especially for large paintings).

Individual compartments designed for drying paintings and for folder storage.

Several alternatives present themselves to the teacher. Open cubbyholes in the room work very well as shown in the illustration on page 9. However, if this facility is not available, a small portable drying rack can be constructed to hold wet paintings. This drying rack, shown in the sketch on this page, is designed to accommodate six paintings at one time. For a class of thirty-six pupils, six of these fit-together units must be constructed. The racks measure 19 x 25 inches (inside) and are designed to store standard 18 x 24 inch sheets of paper; while 25 x 37 inch racks are designed to accommodate the 24 x 36 inch sheets. Larger paintings must be dried on table or counter tops, since drying racks larger than 25 x 37 inches are not practical for most classrooms.

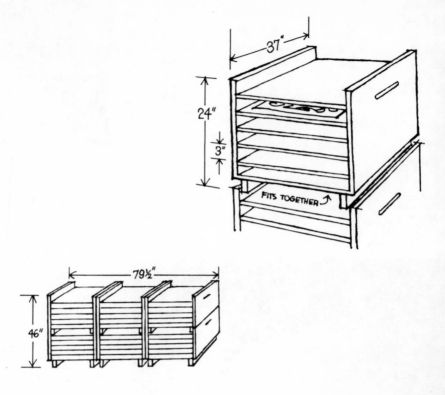

This drying rack is designed to hold 24 x 36 inch paintings (inside dimensions, 25 x 37 inches). These units are planned to accommodate paintings of 30, 36, or 42 pupils (or any number in multiples of six). A smaller unit of the same design may be constructed to hold paintings 18 x 24 inches by making the inside dimensions 19 x 25 inches instead of 25 x 37 inches.

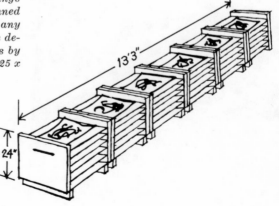

PAINTING TOOLS

It is important to become familiar with the tools and materials for painting. In the sections covering the actual painting experiences, many explanatory statements are given concerning these tools and materials. The following material is meant as reinforcement.

Brushes

Brushes are among the most important tools. Those used in Chapter 9 fall into two main classes: the *flat wash brushes* and the *round-line* or *detail brushes*. The illustrations on page 11 show a range of sizes and shapes in these two categories. The materials used in the manufacture of brushes vary a great deal. Brushes can be made from goat hair, rabbit hair, ox hair, sable, and also from a wide range of synthetic materials. In fact, a few extremists prefer a special brush for painting fine lines made from mouse whiskers! A common brush that most pupils will use is the camel's-hair brush, which oddly enough is not made from camel's hair at all, but squirrel hair.

Although most good brushes will hold their shape and not deteriorate if reasonable care is given them, abuse or rough treatment of even well-made brushes will quickly make them unusable.

Prolonged soaking in water causes moisture to settle under the metal ferrule (the casing that holds bristles to the handle), thus softening the glue and string that hold the hairs together. Prolonged immersion can also cause the varnish finish to peel and crack and finally the wood handle to deteriorate.

Brushes should be cleaned thoroughly in luke-warm water (never hot) after use, then pointed or flattened to the original shape with the fingers. They may be stored, with the bristles up, in a can or suspended, bristles down, without the bristles touching against a solid surface. Care should be taken to see that wet bristles are not jammed or pressed out of shape during storage, as bristles are difficult to reshape when allowed to dry in this manner.

To determine the kind of brush best suited to each specific job, the pupil should experiment for himself. As an example, it would be restrictive to say that a small No. 4 or No. 5 pointed sable brush is always the best brush for lines or details. For some pupils, a No. 12 camel's hair may be just fine for lines and details.

Pupils should be exposed to many painting brushes, including those of different widths, shapes, handle lengths, and bristle compositions.

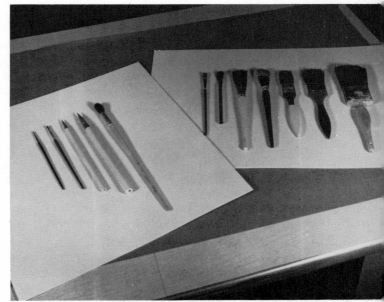

Although it may seem that brushes come in an almost endless variety, there are actually two main types: round or pointed *(left)* and flat *(right).*

Rollers are made from many different materials and come in a variety of sizes. This is a two-inch, soft rubber roller which this pupil finds particularly useful for applying irregular shapes to his painting. A hard-rubber roller or a cloth-covered roller would give entirely different impressions.

Painting Rollers (or brayers)

Rollers used for applying paint are made from many substances. *Fabric covered rollers* (usually made from some form of carpeting) produce a heavier texture than most other rollers.

The most common roller used in painting is the *hard rubber roller*. The core or inner liner is usually made of wood, so it is important when cleaning the roller not to allow it to soak in water for too long a time. Otherwise the ends of the wood core will absorb water, causing them to swell, which will result in "holidays" or bare spots during color applications.

Gelatin rollers are much softer than hard rubber rollers and must be handled with care, especially during storage, since any sharp or rough surface pressed against the gelatin surface will leave a permanent impression in it, making smooth paint application extremely difficult.

Foam rubber or *sponge rubber rollers* have a high paint absorption quality which allows thin, water-soluble paint to be deposited in quantity before resoaking. This is a most versatile paint applicator, since it can be used in several ways. Pressing with the edge forms interesting shapes and lines of varying thicknesses. Rollers should always be washed clean after each painting session.

Painting Spatulas

The painting spatulas, sometimes known as painting knives, come in a variety of styles and shapes ranging from expensive, imported *oil-painting knives* to the inexpensive *pancake spatula* or turner. For student use, the expensive tools are unnecessary. The results achieved with the common pancake spatula, the *flexible-blade putty knife,* or the *dry-wall spatula* compare favorably with those of any other similar painting tool.

For adding details or small sections of color, it may be of value to have several *pointed spatulas,* but this is not absolutely necessary because the end or tip of the pancake spatula can perform this task quite capably.

Other Assorted Painting Tools

Included in this group are *sticks, cardboard, eye droppers,* and even one's *hands* and *fingers.* The pupils' ingenuity will determine the limitations and economy of these supplementary tools. Their characteristics and methods of use are described in other sections of the book.

Paint and Water Receptacles

A most effective palette is a used lunch tray, either the flat, open type or the kind with divided sections, depending on the use. The flat type usually works best for roller painting, while the divided type keeps the colors on the palette separated conveniently for brush painting. Inexpensive metal cookie or muffin tins are also satisfactory when using tempera colors. Water containers can be jars, coffee cans, or mixing bowls. For mixing a batch of powder paint with water, a plastic or enamel bowl is best because it is easy to clean.

PAINTING SURFACES

The painting surfaces referred to in this book fall into two main categories—papers and cardboards with *absorbent* surfaces and those with *non-absorbent, hard* or *glossy finish* surfaces. Other kinds of painting surfaces (other than paper) may work well also. However, their suitability for classroom use is limited because of expense or difficulty in obtaining the quantities necessary for classroom painting experiences. These special surfaces include such materials as fibre board, upson board, acoustical and wall boards.

It may be helpful, at this point, to describe a few of the different characteristics of absorbent and hard-finish papers.

Absorbent Paper

Absorbent papers, or soft papers such as newsprint, rice paper, and construction paper, present special considerations for the pupil. The intensity of paint color may decrease as much as 30 per cent on some kinds of very soft paper. The reason for this is that the color (pigment and water) is absorbed into the paper body rather than remaining on the surface as it does with most hard-finish papers.

Another characteristic of the absorbent papers is that the drying time for paintings is decreased. In addition, soft papers allow a pupil to paint lines or details onto the surface, and then, after allowing the lines to dry, to add washes of various colors over the line design without spreading or lifting them. Although a slight spreading may result in some cases, it can be used to enhance the final result rather than detract from it.

Usually lines become softer or may seem to carry less energy when painted on absorbent surfaces. Here again the pupil should keep in mind the mood he wishes his painting to have and then choose the surface that will best serve this need.

Hard-finish or Non-absorbent Papers

Papers with a hard finish do not allow paint to penetrate as readily as the absorbent papers. The applied paint dries on the surface, thus retaining much more of the original color brilliance.

An advantage of a hard-finish paper is that it allows the pupil to create the impression of energy in his paintings through the use of heavier, bolder lines that do not lose their distinct quality by spreading.

Most papers, other than those that come in rolls, such as butcher paper or wrapping paper, are factory pre-cut and packaged to standard sizes. These sizes usually are 9 x 12, 12 x 18, and 18 x 24 inches. Roll paper, however, can be obtained in many widths. The most convenient widths for classroom use are the 24 and 36 inch rolls. Painting paper in rolls is probably the most economical, but it does require more handling than do the pre-cut packaged papers.

Below are suggestions concerning the suitability of various other painting surfaces to the painting methods described in this book.

Container or box cardboard is an inexpensive, durable, semi-rigid painting surface and works particularly well for spatula painting. This cardboard is usually available from grocery stores (at no cost).

Butcher paper and *patternmaker's paper* (slightly heavier quality) come in rolls varying from 12 inches to 48 inches in width. They take paint well, particularly with the brush and stick methods.

Canvas and canvas board, in prepared form, have applied surface sealers that do

Palettes made from lunch trays provide space for large color deposits and free use of the various tools of exploratory painting.

not easily receive watercolors without a "pulling away" action. However, continued applications of color do adhere and a surface color begins to build up. In *raw* form, canvas needs to be stretched over a frame or tacked over a flat surface, then sealed with latex or other sealer before actual painting. Raw canvas is usually available in rolls 42 inches and 64 inches wide and comes in a variety of weights.

Chipboard has a soft, gray finish and is a heavy, strong, rigid cardboard, ⅛ to ⅙ inch thick. Chipboard is useful for most painting methods but has one drawback in that it bleeds oil spots occasionally because of its composition. It is well adapted to spatula painting.

Construction paper is a versatile paper, soft-surfaced, colored, and it cuts, folds, and tears well. This paper absorbs paint readily; however it buckles if too much moisture is applied. It comes in cut sizes, 9 x 12, 12 x 18, 18 x 24, and 24 x 36 inches. Construction paper is particularly adaptable to block-out painting and brush painting with opaque colors.

Colored tissue paper is translucent, brightly hued, and very fragile. It is most effectively used as a collage-painting material and is available in 20 x 30 inch sheets in packages of 24. Colored tissue paper is brilliant and shows paints well in combination with clear glues and cements.

Manila tag is a durable, all-purpose, cream-colored paper of medium weight. Manila tag takes paint well, has quite high color absorption, and is particularly useful for construction of folders by pupils to hold their painting experiments. It comes in standard sizes.

Masonite is a very heavy, rigid and durable painting surface, but because of inherent oil impregnation in its manufacture it needs to be coated with a sizing such as latex paint. Masonite has a fine surface (one side rough, the other smooth) for spatula and brush painting. It comes in 48x96 inch sheets, ⅛ or ¼ inch thick (usually can be cut to size on request).

Newsprint or newspaper is very porous, absorbs color quickly, and has less sparkle or luster than white paper. It serves the stick and resist methods very well and is quite inexpensive. It comes in standard sizes: 9 x 12, 12 x 18, 18 x 24, and 24 x 36 inches.

Oatmeal paper is a heavy-textured, light-weight painting surface. It is impregnated with woodchips and lends itself to open-surface (background showing through) paintings. Oatmeal paper is particularly adaptable to brush and stick painting. It comes in cut sizes 9 x 12, 12 x 18, and 18 x 24 inches in packages of 100.

Origami paper is a pre-painted, opaque-color paper and is very effective when used in the collage method. Origami paper can be used with transparent or white glues which will tend to dissolve colors as application is made, giving added changes and variations of color. It comes in 6 x 6 inch sheets, 40 sheets to a package, 22 colors.

Pure pulp paper is a basic, first mix paper ordered directly from pulp mills. It is heavily textured in white or natural. It comes in sheets approximately 36 x 36 inches. Pure pulp paper is highly absorbent and readily adaptable to stick painting and brush application. It takes very short runs or washes of color because of its absorbency.

Rice paper is an extremely porous paper, heavily textured with contrasting stringy or opaque lines and semi-transparent areas. Rice paper absorbs paint readily and is particularly effective with stick and brush painting methods. This paper has an unusual tearing and cutting quality which lends itself to collage painting. Usually comes in pre-cut sizes, 18 x 24 inches, in packages of 100.

Shirt liners are available from cleaning and laundering firms. They can be used as test surfaces for roller painting, brush, and stick painting mediums. They come in 8 x 16 inch sheets.

Upson or fibre board is a builder's product with textured surface and is quite adaptable to most painting techniques. It is particularly useful in spatula painting. It comes pre-cut, 18 x 24 inches, or in full sheet form, 48 x 96 inches. Available in ¼ and ⅛ inch thicknesses.

Special watercolor papers are available in many grades and weights. They are machine or hand pressed, textured, and usually white. Watercolor papers insure maximum brilliance of applied colors and can be reworked, erased, sanded, and scraped to change color deposits. They come in varying sizes; 20 x 30 inches is an average sheet.

Illustration board is used by more advanced pupils. It comes in smooth, medium, and rough surfaces and in many weights and grades. Illustration board offers excellent surfaces for any kind of painting. It usually comes in 30 x 40 inch sheets.

PAINTING MEDIUMS

For the purposes of the experiments described in the painting sections of this book, the various paints used are all water-soluble. This is not to suggest, however, that other painting mediums cannot be used successfully in the classroom. Conditions and facilities vary and each teacher needs to determine if other painting mediums can be utilized satisfactorily. For example, if an extremely durable paint is needed, one might mix powdered tempera with shellac or clear varnish. Drying time for this mixture is usually less than one hour. Other mediums might include the latex or rubber-base paints, caseins, and oils. The uppermost consideration when using non-water-soluble mediums is the cleanup of brushes, rollers and other equipment and the need for adequate ventilation for some of the paints and thinners. Some of the most suitable paints are described below.

Powdered tempera colors. These colors are usually non-toxic and are packaged in dry powdered form ready to be mixed with water. A binding agent in the mix allows the color to become fairly durable and free from such problems as cracking or flaking when dry. Colors can be mixed to the proper painting consistency by shaking a quantity of the powder into a small pan and then adding enough water to form a paste. By adding more water, one can obtain the desirable flowing consistency.

In the interest of time economy, it is possible to mix in advance quantities of prepared colors in large containers. Then, by filling plastic squeeze bottles (catsup dispensers) with this mixture the pupil may dispense onto his tray or palette the needed amount of paint. To avoid spoilage and to give the paint a pleasant odor, it is advised that several drops of oil of wintergreen or cloves or a teaspoon of household detergent be added to each 8 oz. container of paint.

Liquid tempera. There is little difference in the costs of liquid tempera and dry tempera of the same quality. However, each type has its own special place in the painting process.

Liquid tempera is ready to use. It is at its ultimate brilliance and nothing is lost by possible improper mixing methods. The colors are usually strong and opaque. Thinning can produce fine color washes without the possible graininess of improperly mixed powder colors. Although a little more expensive than powdered colors, liquid tempera has the advantages of quality and ease of handling. A recent improvement in dispensing has been noted in the adoption by several manufacturers of a plastic container for liquid tempera instead of the glass jars commonly used.

Pan or cake colors. For classroom use, the watercolor sets usually include a range of colors from a minimum selection of at least the three primary colors to as many as sixteen colors in the more complete sets.

There are two different kinds of solid pigments available. One is a transparent medium which leaves the undercolors clearly exposed. The other is the newer opaque color (with more opaque filler) which produces results like those possible with the tempera colors described above.

Boxes containing the cake and pan colors are made from metal and from plastic. The metal boxes have the advantage of ease of storing and of durable construction, while the plastic containers have the advantage of being rust proof.

Water-soluble printing inks. These are available in tubes of several sizes. Colors are quite vivid and they will work very well with the roller painting process. The inks are squeezed out into the lunch tray and spread with the roller to a good working consistency. Overnight drying is usually required for paintings developed with printing inks. Placing paintings near warm air outlets will speed the drying process.

Food or vegetable dye coloring. These colors can be used instead of thinned-out watercolor to achieve brilliant color effects. They are rather expensive if used to cover large areas. They are particularly effective on rice paper. In some cases the food-dye colors have a tendency to fade after a period of time.

There are no rigid rules or formulas for using any of the above color mediums. For example, an opaque medium can become a transparent medium if enough water is added, and transparent colors will become opaque if the application is made heavy enough or if repeated overlays of color are applied.

Synthetic Media. A recent development in synthetic water-soluble paint is the new polymer-medium tempera, which is now becoming available for classroom use.

These paints have several of the special advantages of oils and caseins without some of their limitations—mainly, the long drying time and cracking of the older mediums. Polymer medium is water-soluble during the actual painting process. However, the finished paintings are extremely durable, highly resistant to cracking and flaking. Permanent drying time for the polymer medium is dependent only on the rate of evaporation of the water from the painted surface. Lightly painted surfaces will become dry in just a few minutes. (Some care should be taken in cleanup of painting tools, since this medium does not dissolve after drying.)

1. Cardboard Painting

The use of cardboard as a painting tool is a development that promises to provide inspiration to many. The cardboard method has special advantages for water-soluble paints. In watercolor or tempera painting cut or torn cardboard shapes offer the pupil a method of color application very different in results from techniques using the brush.

The method illustrated here is for painting large flat areas or shapes. Color is poured onto the palette (in this case a tray) and mixed with a spreader. The cut or torn cardboard shapes are pressed into the color. The cardboard, laden with paint, is then pressed onto the painting surface. Because of the pressure applied when transferring the paint, a textured surface is produced. The unequal distribution of paint in this method creates a pleasing informal effect. This in itself is stimulating to the young pupil, since he is usually not too concerned with entirely accurate representation.

A complete composition may be developed by cutting or tearing out a variety of cardboard shapes to fill in the total painting surface. To further develop or overpaint the picture, more cardboard shapes must be prepared for successive color changes and overlays.

A distinct advantage of this method of painting is that very little undercolor, or first color, is spread or removed by subsequent applications. Paint applied by pressing does not have a tendency to run or lift as it does when applied with a brush. Added differences in results are influenced by other factors: absorbency and texture of paper, consistency of paint, and pressure applied to the cardboard shapes.

In addition, the edge of the cardboard is one of the most effective line painting tools available. Using a variety in thickness and flexibility of cardboard shapes, the pupil will be able to form an almost endless number of curves, angles, and thicknesses of line. The cardboard edge may be skived, shaved or even blunted with a heavy object. A small mallet or hammer is excellent for this purpose.

The colors for a line design may be prepared in the same manner as previously described for the flat cardboard shapes. The prepared cardboard edge is pressed into the paint and then transferred to the painting surface. Successive pressings will develop a variety of linear and textural results not readily achieved by a brush or some other method of application.

There are several suggested alternate ways to develop paintings using the cardboard method. A pupil may start with the line or cardboard edge design and then apply background color with flat cardboard shapes, filling in the areas created by the line design. In contrast, the pupil may reserve the use of the cardboard edge method as the finishing touch or final details of the painting. This is usually the most effective procedure and is illustrated in the accompanying demonstration. By experimenting, the pupil will determine his own combinations to most effectively portray his thoughts.

Tool cleanup is held to a minimum, as the cardboard shapes are disposable—a distinct advantage over many other methods of painting.

MATERIALS

Cardboard (various sizes, thicknesses)
Chip carving knife (for older pupils)
Paper cutter (for teacher use)
Scissors
Palette (large tray)
Water-soluble paint
Mallet or hammer
Painting surface, flexible or rigid (paper, cardboard)

Cutting out cardboard shapes with scissors. Assorted sizes and thicknesses of cardboard should be available.

Preparing the paint. To insure proper consistency, the pupil may add powdered clay and a small quantity of school paste to the tempera. Water is used to thin the paint. A cardboard spatula works well as a mixing tool.

The first cardboard shape is pressed into the prepared paint. A firm pressure will insure complete paint coverage. Excess paint at the edges will not detract from the finished painting.

The paint-laden cardboard shape is pressed upon the painting surface according to the design that the pupil has in mind.

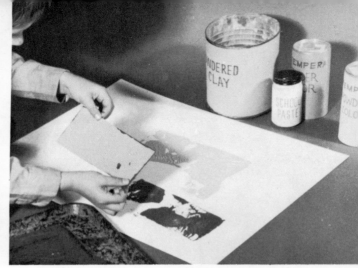

A characteristic result of this method of paint application is an uneven deposit of paint within each shape. These uneven deposits should not be considered flaws, as the overall result makes use of this interesting texture.

Another cardboard shape is applied, using a second color.

As the pupil proceeds, he applies more colors and shapes to his painting, filling in the background by using smaller shapes to develop a general color pattern and texture. Further mixing of color in the tray should be limited to the amount necessary for these smaller shapes.

The pupil is now ready to apply linear details to his painting. To accomplish this, additional cardboard shapes are cut to lengths and, if desired, pounded slightly with a hammer or similar tool to provide a variety in thickness and shape to the line design. For curved lines, the cardboard is formed by bending.

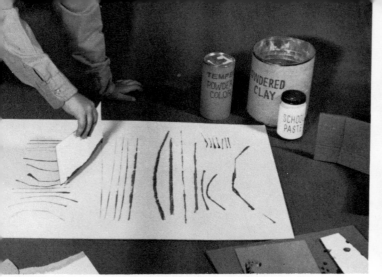

Linear design is achieved by pressing the edge of the cardboard into the paint in the tray and then transferring it to the painting surface. It is sometimes desirable to try out this process first on a practice sheet.

By repeating this process, using a variety of shapes, curved lines, straight lines, and thick and thin lines, the pupil can finish his painting with as little or as much detail he feels is necessary. It is important to have several trays of color available for the line-design application to insure a variety in the finishing stages of the painting.

Finished painting

EXAMPLES OF CARDBOARD PAINTING

Combined cardboard and spatula

Combined cardboard and brush

2. Squeegee and Sponge Painting

This method of painting permits, as its particular advantage, speed in applying paint to the painting surface. Large areas of color may be applied with little concern for detail or the eventual break up of space into its smaller segments.

Special preparation for this painting experience includes providing a large tray on which to mix colors. Any water-soluble colors are suitable. Liquid and powdered tempera are particularly adaptable. The painting tools can range from a simple cardboard squeegee and an inexpensive sponge to a commercially produced small window cleaning sponge and squeegee which are reasonably inexpensive.

For the pupil to be able to work satisfactorily with this method, the painting surface must be placed firmly upon a smooth table top, preferably with the corners taped down to prevent slipping during the squeegeeing process. The paper surface should be strong enough to withstand the scraping and sponging actions of the tools. The purpose of the large flat tray is to afford the pupil maneuverability while mixing colors. An ample tray will also allow the pupil to mix variations of a color within his palette rather than having to clean up between colors.

One of the distinctive features of this method of painting is the spontaneous surface quality of the work. The large color masses have a fresh quality rather than the sometimes labored appearance produced with a brush.

After the pupil has determined the theme for his painting, he is ready to apply the first colors to the painting surface. This is done by saturating one side of the sponge by pressing it into the wet color. Then by applying the sponge to the general area selected on the painting surface, the pupil can deposit any quantity of color desired depending upon the pressure exerted on the sponge. The area of color deposited should be considerably less than the space it is eventually going to fill. Then, with a squeegee of an appropriate size, the pupil may spread this wet color in a sliding or scraping motion to the extremes of the shape he has planned for this particular color. An interesting surface pattern tends to develop during this process because wherever the squeegee is allowed to come to a stop, a heavier deposit of color results. Thus, within each shape there will be several planes and lines of varying weights and thicknesses.

After some of the major areas of the composition have been filled in, the pupil may wish to squeegee a contrasting color over or beyond areas already filled in. This method works well because the squeegee process forces the overlay colors to be applied thinly. The heavier the pressure of the squeegee, the less dense is the color applied, thus allowing interesting overlays of color. This permits the underpainting to play an important role in the finished work. If a line design is desired, it is a simple matter to use the edge of the squeegee or any fairly sharp cardboard edge to press lines into the desired shapes or lengths with a stamping motion.

The painting surface will play a determining role in the results possible with the squeegee and sponge process. Heavily textured paper will allow raised portions of the paper to absorb more color than the low areas, thus providing additional texture to the painting. Smooth, soft-surface paper will absorb color at a higher rate, resulting in heavier color deposits. Smooth, hard paper will usually result in a longer run of color, more transparency, and greater success with overlays of color. Since all paints recommended for use in this method are water-soluble, it is important that all pigment be thoroughly rinsed from sponges and squeegees after each painting session. Sponges, especially, deteriorate quickly when hard deposits of tempera are allowed to remain for any period of time.

MATERIALS
Sponges (variety of sizes and shapes)
Squeegee (commercial or handmade)
Cardboard (assorted shapes and thicknesses)
Palette (any large tray)
Paint—water-soluble tempera (dry or liquid)
Water
Clean-up materials—paper towels, rags
Painting surfaces—butcher, kraft, or construction paper

A variety of sponges and squeegees.

Cutting cardboard to use as extra squeegees. It is desirable to cut a variety of sizes and shapes.

Several colors poured into flat lunch trays may be shared by a number of pupils at the same time.

A sponge is dipped into the paint, which should be of a moderately thick consistency. The paint may be applied with a sweeping motion or daubed.

The first large areas are sponged onto the painting. A squeegee (or sponge) could be used to apply the initial color. The pupil should be encouraged to create as many textures as possible, since this is one of the keys to successful sponge painting.

The squeegee is used to spread the color, and thus create exciting color movements and textures.

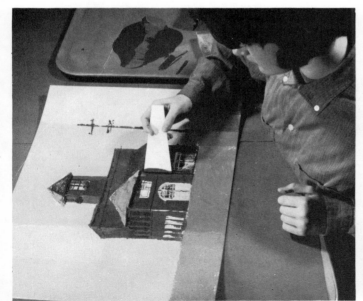

Smaller "hand-fashioned" squeegees can be used to paint the smaller areas and to add further details.

The edge of the cardboard may be used for linear effects. These "details" will be of a spontaneous nature, indicating the freedom and vitality of squeegee and sponge painting.

The finished painting.

EXAMPLES OF SQUEEGEE AND SPONGE PAINTING
(See also Color, page 27)

Combined sponge, squeegee and cardboard

Combined sponge, squeegee and spatula

Combined sponge, squeegee and cardboard

3. Collage Painting

This method challenges the pupil with a variety of surface materials instead of the single painting surface most commonly used in painting.

Collage painting might well be called the "layer" or "sandwich" method. By gluing layers of paper or related materials to the original foundation, or first layer, the pupil builds up overlapping planes and shapes. The addition of paint, as the collage progresses, soon produces the combinations of textures and colors that form a collage painting. Several glues and pastes work well as adhering agents. Particularly effective are the white casein base glues that are frequently packaged in plastic squeeze-bottle containers. These white glues dry clear and do not stain the painting surface. The containers are usually equipped with dispensing heads which allow small amounts of glue to be spread at one time in the desired areas. The glue can also be applied with a brush or one's finger. Some of the collage paper materials, such as the colored tissue papers, are quite thin and sometimes difficult to paste to the surface or paint on without tearing. When eventually pasted down, these torn papers will not detract from the painting but frequently enhance the finished work.

The collage-painting process allows the pupil to select surface colors in a variety of materials of great textural and color diversity, and to combine them to make paintings that have real depth. These paintings may be further developed by the addition of a line design on top of, or between, the applied surface color layers.

However, quite frequently the overlapping of semi-transparent papers will create linear effects without the actual application of lines over the color areas.

It is exciting to vary the impact of collage painting by the application of wet color (tempera) in strategic areas as a foil to succeeding layers of transparent surface materials, such as colored tissue or rice paper. The quick absorption of color through these thin materials often results in a softening or spreading effect of the color. However, the pupil may if desired re-emphasize these softer areas. This he can readily do by applying additional opaque color (paint or paper) directly over the dry or wet undercolor wherever necessary.

The method of preparing the different overlays of collage materials may vary. However, there are two methods which offer distinctly different characteristics: cutting the surface materials and tearing them. Cutting with scissors or knife will result in a precise, hard-line effect, while tearing the materials will lend a softer and less rigid quality to the surface. Wetting the paper either through the gluing process or by adding paint will sometimes change the color of the surface material itself. Spreading or dissolving colors in the paper will usually blend with applied color or fade from the original color of the applied paper. This method of painting needs to be explored by the pupil so that he may discover for himself how to combine the various approaches into a successful painting experience.

There are several variations of this method. As we have noted, torn edges of paper may be contrasted with cut edges of paper. Wet colors may be applied under or over applied surface materials. Still another variation is to begin the painting on a heavier cardboard surface material. Certain types of cardboards are composed of many layers of paper pressed together to form a heavier, stable surface. The pupil may score or cut into areas of his composition and peel away portions of the original painting. These exposed areas are again ready to accept additional paint. The inner layers of paper are usually of a coarse or softer consistency and will absorb wet paint more readily than the outer or harder pressed top layers. This imparts a distinctively different appearance to the painted areas. Exploration with many types of cardboard will result in additional variations on the collage painting process described above.

MATERIALS

Powdered or liquid tempera
Scissors, paper cutter or cutting blade
Glue or paste (squeeze-bottle container preferred)
Collage materials (tissue, rice paper, construction paper, tracing paper)
Brushes (for glue application and for painting)
Cardboard painting surfaces (varying thicknesses)
Palette (lunch tray)
Water

Japanese colored tissue paper, sheets of colored construction paper, and other interesting papers may be included for selection.

Cutting tissue-paper shapes with scissors to paste onto the painting surface.

Rice paper can be torn for use in the collage painting. Torn edges usually form interesting shapes, different in character from cut shapes.

Applying glue to the painting surface before attaching pieces of paper.

Positioning colored tissue paper.

Gluing the tissue into position. The paper may be rubbed so that it lies flat.

Combined squeegee and sponge painting

Collage with brush details

28

Brushing color over one of the tissue shapes. Color can be applied at any stage in the development of the collage painting.

Smaller shapes can be applied over existing papers and painted areas depending on the final result the pupil wishes to achieve.

Finishing touches are added with paint and tissue.

The finished painting.

EXAMPLES OF COLLAGE PAINTING
(See also Color, page 27)

Collage variation

Combined brush and pencil

Combined newspaper and colored tissue

4. Block-out Painting

The block-out method of painting borrows from the screen printing and the stencil processes characteristics which have a special application to painting. It is a method that provides the pupil with a means of adding a distinctive textural quality to his work by using a screen.

The only tools needed are cardboard of various thicknesses and sizes to be used as the paint applicators and screening material, such as crinoline, tarlatan, cheesecloth or window screening. Although masking tape and wax paper are sometimes used to block out specific areas of the design, it is usually quite effective to work without a rigid template, directly on selected areas of the painting surface by merely moving a portable section of screen over the composition.

While the usual screen printing process produces a number of identical prints, paintings developed by the pupil with this method are definitely one-of-a-kind creations.

Block-out painting offers the excitement of surprise and suspense, since one cannot determine in advance the exact textural quality that will result from each individual color that is applied.

After determining his composition, the pupil may apply the large masses of color with one of two methods: (1) A mixture of paint in a tray may be scooped up with a cardboard squeegee and applied through the screen with a sliding or spreading motion within the outlines of the shapes designed, or (2) the designed shape may be cut from cardboard in advance and pressed by hand into the prepared pigment (evenly spread on the palette or tray) and then transferred onto the painting surface by hand pressing directly through the screen. Either method works well and each imparts a distinct quality to the finished work.

Particularly interesting effects can be obtained with overlapping applications of color. The screening material usually blocks out some portion of the color (the screen prevents all of the color from passing through). This results in an interesting color separation or exposure of the "under" color (the preceding, already applied color). It is possible to develop other variations of this method by having the pupil experiment with an application of wet color over a previous color that has not yet dried. This will cause a blending of colors, quite different in surface quality from wet color applied over dry color.

A variety of screens may be provided for the pupil. Crinoline or surgical gauze gives a uniform, even textural quality, while cheesecloth, window screening or other wide-mesh fabrics will produce rougher textural surfaces. For ease of control, these screening materials may be mounted in cardboard, although the screen fabric can be used without any supporting frame. The choice might be determined by the method of paint application used. A sliding or spreading motion with a cardboard squeegee would be used best with a framed screen, while pressing the color by hand through the screen would not require a frame.

Screening materials have varying degrees of durability. Surgical gauze and similar materials contain stiffening agents like starch which disappear with exposure to any prolonged use of water-soluble materials. Plastic-base, open-surfaced fabrics are not affected in this manner and are not of such temporary or short-lived construction.

If the pupil wishes to develop a heavy-surfaced painting similar to an oil painting, he may add a small amount of powdered clay to the tempera paint. This creates a thicker and heavier consistency. A thicker mixture has a tendency to clog the screening material quite readily, especially if the screen is of a finer weave or mesh. However, the screen may be washed between applications to prolong its effective use. It should be noted that as more clay is added, the color of the mixture becomes less brilliant in hue.

Where small areas of color are desired, color may be pressed through the screen with the finger. In fact, this method can be used with rather interesting results to

Rectangular panels of different sizes are cut from card-board boxes.

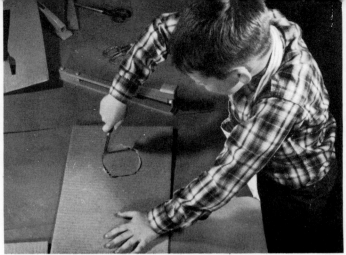

Cutting an opening in a cardboard panel. Care should be taken to protect tabletops, and pupils, from carelessly used cutting tools.

complete the entire painting. Another variation that may be tried is painting directly upon the screen, then pressing the wet screen to the paper.

For line designs, the pupil may press the paint-laden edge of a piece of board through the screen. These lines will appear broken or separated; however, they are usually strong enough to carry the desired linear effect.

The predominant textural quality of paintings developed by the block-out method distinguishes them from those made with other methods, particularly such methods as painting with a brush.

A more defined shape is cut out. Scissors can also be used to cut shapes and openings.

MATERIALS

Powdered or liquid tempera
Powdered clay
Scissors and paper cutter
Masking tape
Wax paper or stencil paper
Cardboard—assorted shapes and thicknesses
Crinoline, cheesecloth, or other porous fabrics
Palettes (lunch trays)
Bowls or water containers
Water
Painting surfaces (paper, cardboard)

The pupil may not always have a specific plan in mind when cutting shapes into the cardboard, so it is well to have a variety of sizes to work with.

Crinoline is cut into sizes large enough to cover the openings in the cardboard panels. Any gauze-type material will do if crinoline is not available.

Stapling the crinoline over the opening.

Masking tape is also convenient to use for fastening the crinoline to the cardboard.

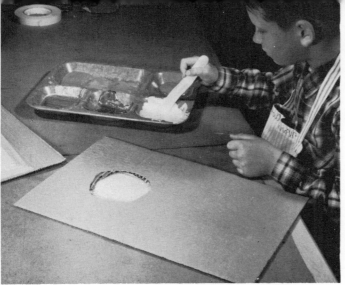

Mixing the paint preparatory to applying it to the painting surface through the opening in the cardboard.

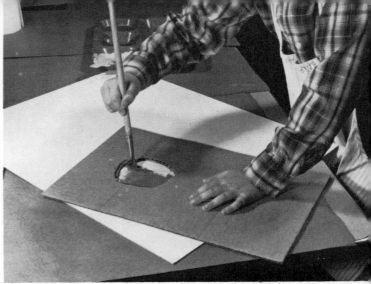

Applying the paint. The paint should be of fairly thick consistency, as thin, watery paint will run beyond or under the crinoline covered cut out area.

No real attempt should be made to create exact or refined shapes. The "crude" shapes have an interesting quality.

Developing the painting by applying more paint and overlapping some of the shapes.

The finished painting.

Combined block-out, cardboard and brush

EXAMPLES OF BLOCK-OUT PAINTING

Combined block-out and spatula painting

Block-out on colored construction paper

5. Spatula Painting

The spatula, the painting knife, and the plaster spreader are highly successful painting tools for pupils.

Paintings developed with a spatula are characterized by a naturally heavier paint deposit than those achieved by almost any other method.

Powdered tempera, the paint recommended for this method, works well in spatula painting when mixed to the consistency of mayonnaise. Powdered tempera mixed with prepared laundry starch makes a very satisfactory mixture. Still another good combination of similar consistency is liquid tempera and powdered clay.

A heavy painting medium that is very adaptable to spatula painting because of its thicker consistency is the new polymer tempera. This new paint is water soluble. It is recommended that polymer medium paint may prove best adapted to pupils who have first explored spatula painting with other mixtures.

When applying paint with a spatula, the pupil may begin to build up layers or deposits of color in much the same way that an oil or casein painting is developed. A thicker or heavier textural quality is the chief characteristic of this method. The degree of the painting's roughness will also be determined by the kind and size of spatula used.

Spatulas may take several different forms. For instance, a very effective and versatile painting tool is the common pan-cake turner. Pupils may bring discarded spatulas from home or purchase inexpensive ones at hardware or variety stores. Another useful tool that may double as a painting spatula is the plasterer's (drywall) flexible-blade putty knife. These spatulas and knives, together with spatulas specifically made for painting, which come in a variety of lengths and widths, will provide the pupil with ample painting tools for experimentation.

With all spatulas, it is important to select only those with flexible blades. The end of the spatula (the last inch or so) possesses this spring-like quality. This flexibility is important because the spatula method of paint application requires a painting tool that can slide, press, and manipulate the paint on the painting surface to provide the most interesting and exciting textural effects possible. If the blade is rigid, as is the case with most putty knives, these interesting results cannot be achieved nearly as well.

The painting surface required for spatula painting should be somewhat stronger and more rigid than that used for most of the painting methods described elsewhere. Since some degree of pressure is necessary when paint is applied, it is advisable to use a heavy cardboard, upson board, or wallboard for the painting surface in order to minimize the possibility of bending or creasing the painting surface, which may loosen or crack the heavy deposits of paint.

When beginning the painting, it is best to fill in the large areas of the composition first. If time allows, the entire painting surface should be covered. Following this, the painting can be completed by adding the smaller areas and the details. This second step may have to occur on the following day, as the large, thick background areas sometimes do not dry fast enough to permit completion in one session.

Overpainting with a spatula is a fine method of creating surface color changes that have depth. This type of painting creates little mounds and crevices or "highs" and "lows" on the painting surface. When this uneven surface is dry, succeeding applications of paint will tend to cover the original paint in some areas and "slide over" or expose other areas, depending upon whether these surfaces are high or low. The low impressions are sometimes referred to as the negative or low-texture areas, while the raised or higher surfaces may be called the positive or raised-texture areas. The pupil may develop added richness in color and develop variety in surfaces by applying several succeeding spreads of color (perhaps three or four colors or more) in selected portions of his painting.

The spatula has the added advantage as a painting tool of providing an excellent means to manipulate heavy or thick colors. For example, thick color may be applied to the painting and spread with the spatula to a stop or edge, leaving a small ridge or mound of paint. These ridges can be

Spatulas of various kinds. A kitchen spatula is being tested for flexibility.

Preparing the paint. A mixture of powdered clay, tempera, and water will insure a thick consistency. Either powder tempera or liquid tempera works well in combination with powdered clay.

A heavy box cardboard, chipboard, illustration board, or upson board is necessary because a thinner paper will tend to be difficult to handle as the paint is being applied.

Mixing the desired color on the palette.

effectively incorporated into the design and surface texture. Color applied with a spatula also has the advantage of remaining within the desired areas of the painting and not running or spreading beyond these areas.

An interesting variation may be accomplished by blending colors with the spatula. This is done by applying one wet color into another wet color, thus mixing colors directly on the painting surface. It is well to re-emphasize that paintings developed

with the spatula method usually require a somewhat longer drying period than paintings developed by other methods. However, even a moderately heavy-painted surface will dry sufficiently overnight.

Spatula painting has the particular

The first color is applied to the painting surface.

Large areas are laid on in a broad, sweeping manner using as many colors as necessary.

The edge of the spatula, as well as the flat surface, can be used to spread the paint to achieve various results.

Here the pupil applies the paint in a stamping motion with the edge of the blade, creating interesting irregular lines.

Finishing touches are applied with a smaller palette knife. In order to maintain a spontaneous feeling, a broad, sweeping, and rapid approach should be encouraged.

merit for the pupil of providing a close approximation of the experience of oil painting or casein painting but with much less expense and difficulty of preparation. The heavy textural quality of spatula painting is a distinctive characteristic.

MATERIALS

Spatulas (variety of sizes and shapes)
Paint (powdered tempera, liquid tempera)
Thickening agents (powdered clay, laundry starch)
Palette (large tray, flat surface)
Painting surfaces (cardboard, chipboard, wallboard, upson board or any fairly rigid surface material)

EXAMPLES OF SPATULA PAINTING

Combined spatula and stick

The finished painting.

Combined spatula, squeegee, and cardboard

Combined spatula and brush

6. Resist Painting

Resist painting is a unique and fascinating technique relying on the principle that water and wax (or other resist medium) will not mix. It is important that the resist medium be incompatible with water or water-soluble paints. Resist media include ordinary colored crayons, liquid wax, and various cements. Water-soluble paints may consist of tempera, transparent watercolor or ordinary food coloring. When the paint is applied over a design or texture in a resist medium, the paint pulls away and refuses to remain over the resisting areas. However, the paint readily soaks into the paper in the spaces not covered by the resist medium. This exciting painting technique almost invariably brings with it some degree of success and satisfaction.

One of the simplest resist media with which pupils may experiment is the ordinary wax crayon. The choice of assorted colors will alter the appearance of the finished painting. Some colored crayons produce startling results when combined with an overpainting of contrasting watersoluble paints. White is a particularly effective crayon; in combination with colored over-washes, it produces paintings of strong contrast and dramatic impact.

When the pupil has determined the idea for his painting, he may set about laying out his composition with a wax crayon. Both line design and texture can be developed satisfactorily with the crayon. After the crayon work is finished, the paint is added in washes or patterns over the entire paper or in selected areas. Later, the pupil may add more wet color over previously painted areas. It should be noted that the initial wax lines and areas will allow the paper or painting surface to play an important role in the finished work. However, the crayon may also be applied over dried areas of painted color. Since these areas of color will usually be darker than the original painting surface, the applied wax will produce a less distinctive contrast or a less strong resist than when applied initially to the white paper.

An interesting variation can be obtained with the use of a new water-soluble wax resist medium. This liquid wax may be applied to the painting surface in a number of ways: (1) The pupil may trail his resist design with liquid wax by squeezing it onto the painting surface from an eye dropper. The resulting quality of the line or texture will be determined by the amount of pressure applied to the bulb of the eye dropper and by the degree of movement of the eye dropper over the painting surface. A slow, deliberate pace by the pupil will allow more liquid wax to be deposited and result in a wider line. A faster movement will result in a finer, more delicate line design. (2) The liquid wax may also be applied quite satisfactorily with a stick or brush. Brushes used with liquid wax should be washed thoroughly.

It should be noted that the heavier liquid wax deposits will have a tendency to turn amber or light brown when they dry. However, with practice the pupil can determine the necessary pace at which he needs to work to minimize this characteristic of dried liquid wax.

After the crayon or liquid wax resist has been applied to the painting surface, it may be altered in a number of ways: (1) The pupil may scratch through the applied wax, thus exposing the porous paper surface. Paint added later will be absorbed into these scratched or tooled areas making other lines or textures. (2) He may use a flat tool to shave off the wax with a shoveling motion. (3) The pupil may explore another variation by crumpling or creasing the painting, producing crevices into which added paint will be absorbed. (4) The pupil may also design with a resist material directly on selected portions of newspapers, thus leaving exposed the printed word in the design.

Other painting materials that resist water-soluble paints quite readily include rubber cement and a variety of plastic-base or casein-base glues. In addition, food dye may be used full strength or mixed with water to make beautiful, vivid colors which emerge between the applied resist media.

Resist painting has the element of surprise or suspense as its strong quality. This begins with the pupil's initial application of paint over a resisting surface design and occurs again with the emergence and separation of color from the resist—a very exciting experience.

MATERIALS

Crayons (wax, all colors and white)
Liquid wax (water base, available at most ceramic supply houses)
Eye dropper (or sticks for applying liquid wax)
Tempera (liquid or powdered)
Watercolors (transparent)
Painting brushes (flat wash type)
Painting surface (butcher paper, construction paper, newspapers)
Food coloring (assorted colors)

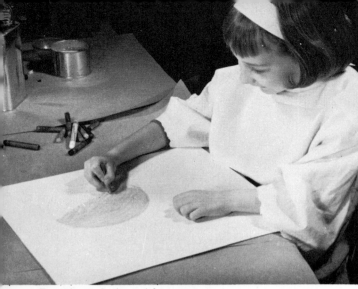

Drawing a design with wax crayons.

The drawing is developed further.

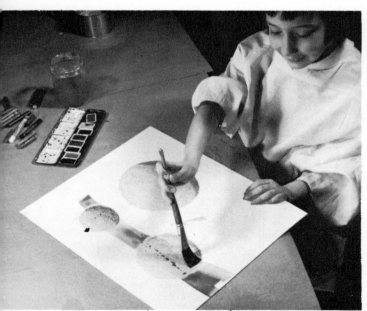

A watercolor wash is being applied over the entire area. The paint is "accepted" by the paper and "resisted" by the wax crayon areas. A large, flat brush is used for the large areas.

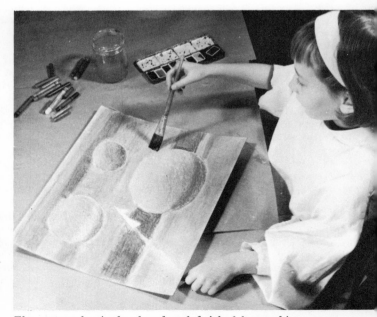

The watercolor is developed and finished by working some darker colors into the desired areas.

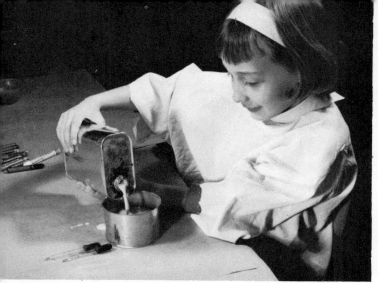

Liquid, water-soluble wax is poured into a small can so that the eye dropper can be filled.

Applying wax to the painting surface with the eye dropper to form a design.

After the wax has dried and watercolor has been applied in a wash, the wax is scraped off, revealing the white paper underneath. The white areas thus become a line design.

It is sometimes desirable to work back into the design with crayon after the painting is dry.

The completed painting. Many watercolor hues were used by the pupil to achieve a colorful design.

EXAMPLES OF RESIST PAINTING

Brush and crayon resist painting

Oil-wax crayon and brush resist painting

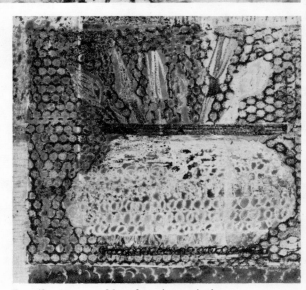

Pencil, crayon and brush resist variation

7. Roller Painting

The roller provides the pupil with a versatile tool for developing paintings. Rollers, or brayers, come in a variety of sizes and surface densities (hardness or softness of the rubber covering). Rollers can be used in many ways. For example, to create a line design the roller is tipped on edge and rolled onto the paper. For heavy or dense areas of painting, the roller is applied flat and rolled directly on the surface. If additional smaller but distinct areas of paint application are desired, the roller is brought into contact with the paper in a dabbing or stamping motion.

A distinctive feature of roller painting is that large areas of color in the painting may be applied in a wide band with a single run of the roller. The applied color will tend to produce a progressive change in texture as the roller is gradually depleted of color. The first contact with the paper surface with a paint-laden roller produces the heaviest color deposit. As the roller is moved further along the color becomes progressively thinner or lighter. Of particular interest in this method is the possibility of color changes from overlapping applications of paint. To provide additional sensitive areas in his painting, the pupil may purposely plan to deposit a lighter application of paint over previously developed dense applications, thus producing an interesting play of under color which shows through.

A roller painting has the remarkable inherent characteristic of being able to show depth through the natural use of crossing or overlapping runs of paint. The pupil can control the degree of contrast and color separation by using heavier or thinner paint mixtures and by varying the methods of loading the roller with paint.

Roller painting permits several different methods of paint preparation. By mixing powdered or liquid tempera with laundry starch or powdered clay, a rather thin paint can take on a heavier consistency which is ideally suited to application with a roller. It should be noted that the original brilliance of color may be dulled somewhat when starch or clay is added. Wheat paste may also be added to tempera as a thickening agent.

Another medium that works quite successfully with the roller is water-soluble printing ink. An advantage is the fact that it is usually premixed to the proper consistency for roller application. Since inks are more brilliant than tempera colors, a higher degree of bright color is usually retained in the finished painting. A disadvantage is that printing inks take a long time to dry.

In this method of painting, textural differences seem to be influenced most by the consistency of the paint. A thin or watery paint applied on paper with a roller will result in a surface quality very different from that produced by a mixture of heavy, paste-like paint. The roller itself responds to each mixture differently and the pupil will soon discover the consistency most satisfactory for him.

The palette or paint container should have a flat bottom, and be large enough to permit the roller to pick up enough paint to make a wide run of color. A speckled or textured paint surface may be achieved by rolling the paint-laden roller over a rough surface—such as paper toweling, the side of a brick, sandpaper, canvas, or even coarse-grained or rough wood—before applying it to the paper.

Paint may be rolled out onto heavy cardboard, rigid plastic, hard-surfaced wallboard, or glass. Turkish toweling spread out in a tray and saturated with paint works well also. Several colors should be available for the pupil at the same time, and several sizes of rollers should be provided to allow for as many interchanges of shapes and colors as possible.

Many commercially fabricated rollers are inexpensive. However, a handmade roller may do as well. An adequate roller may be fashioned by covering a discarded spool with rubber (tube patching or rubber hose) and attaching a handle made from a metal coat hanger. Wooden doweling inserted into a length of rubber hose also works well. In addition, larger commercial rollers may be cut down to smaller sizes to provide the variety of sizes needed. It is important to protect the roller's rubber surface; it should be rinsed well after each painting session.

The most distinguishing characteristic of roller painting is the overlapping planes and color fadeouts. In addition, fine lines and heavier, coarse lines are produced by increased or decreased pressure applied to the roller. By experimenting with this method of painting, the pupil will gain control of this versatile tool. For many pupils this accomplishment will give added assurance and encourage further exploration.

MATERIALS

Assorted rollers (variety of sizes and densities)

Paint (thickened tempera)

Ink (water-soluble printing ink, tube)

Palette (lunch tray, toweling, plastic, masonite, or glass)

Painting surfaces (butcher paper, newspapers, construction paper, rice paper, drawing paper)

Thickening agents (powdered clay, starch, school paste)

An assortment of rollers—commercial and handmade.

Liquid tempera paint being poured into the palette. Powdered tempera may also be used. A fine medium, if available, is water-soluble printers' ink, which rolls beautifully but takes longer to dry.

Rolling the paint to the proper consistency.

Testing the consistency of the paint by a trial on paper toweling.

The large color areas are applied. The paint need not be rolled out flat and thin, but may be more effective if the ridges and textures are allowed to remain on the painting surface.

The edge of a roller is used to paint a linear design over larger background areas of color.

EXAMPLES OF ROLLER PAINTING
(See also Frontispiece)

The finished painting.

Roller painting

Roller painting

Roller painting

Roller painting

Roller and cardboard

8. Stick Painting

As the name implies, this technique employs a wooden stick as the means of applying paint.

The painting surface can be almost any kind of paper. On slick or hard-surfaced papers, the paint remains as applied without spreading. Rough-surfaced or soft-surfaced papers will offer a contrasting result. When the paper is highly absorbent, the paint will spread more.

The pupil may develop his painting in several ways: (1) He may wet the paper surface with clear water, then, while the paper is still damp, dip the stick into paint and apply it directly to the paper. Colors thus applied will spread quickly, forming interesting larger areas. This wet-paper method will not retain fine lines even when the paint is applied with the edge of the stick. (2) If the painting surface is not dampened beforehand, the paint will not run and spread as much. Therefore, resulting color areas will develop into more rigid shapes, areas, and lines rather than larger, spread-out areas of color.

Additional combinations of these two methods can develop into a third kind of stick painting. By applying wet paint with the stick to pre-dampened paper for the large areas of color and then allowing these colors to dry, the pupil can later develop an overlay-line design on top of the dried color areas. Since the second "coat" is applied over a dry color surface, the resulting characteristics will form a pleasing contrast with the original wet applications underneath.

It is not necessary to sharpen sticks for applying paint with this method. An edge or corner is found on all sticks, and by tilting the paint-laden stick slightly as one would a brush, the exposed edge of the stick will work much like a pointed brush. By experimenting with sticks made from many kinds of wood, the pupil will soon learn which to use for the best results in a particular kind of painting. Chinese chop sticks or other sticks made from bamboo work well as do balsa-wood sticks, which have a very high paint absorption characteristic. Since hardwood sticks do not absorb paint readily, the initial application of paint with these sticks will be quite bold and heavy. A pupil should prepare many sticks of a variety of sizes and kinds of woods so that he may explore their individual characteristics as paint applicators. The sticks may be used over and over again and are inexpensive painting tools for the pupil.

By experimentation, the pupil will see what happens when the paint is prepared quite thin and, by contrast, what happens when it is used with a paint mixture about the consistency of heavy cream. He will soon see what changes develop in his work and he may become more selective in his choice of sticks and paint mixtures.

Exploring the possibilities of different papers is also important. Rice paper, for instance, is highly absorbent and somewhat irregular in its texture. Paint applied with a stick on rice paper or any other absorbent paper will spread quickly in some areas and will remain as applied, without spreading, in other denser areas of the paper. Other papers such as oatmeal, tissue, and newsprint will also absorb and spread paint readily. Old newspapers provide an excellent painting surface for stick painting. The ink-printed surface on the newspaper will partially resist some of the applied paint. This resistance also works well as a means for providing a textural background of interest and variety that can be incorporated into the design.

Background colors may be applied in a rather watery state so that ample spreading can take place. However, a line design that the pupil wishes to be quite definite may be applied with thicker paint.

Another interesting variation to explore is to use several bottom layers of paper when painting with a thin or watery paint solution. The soaking through of the applied design provides the pupil with two, three, or more rather rough, crude paintings. These may then be developed further by adding detail. Still another way to produce a variation of the above process is for the pupil to apply paint to the overall design in one application without allowing it to dry. Then, by placing a clean sheet of paper over this wet painting and rubbing the top sheet, a reverse transfer of the original painting is made. This transfer usually has a less sharp quality not found in the original.

The paint itself need not be mixed on a palette as with other methods, but rather in small cups, tuna fish cans, frozen juice cans, or muffin tins. Since the sticks need to be dipped into the paint, some depth in the containers is desirable.

Stick painting has the advantage of economical application and uniqueness of line design in combination with background patterns. The spreading of paint by absorption is a distinctive feature. This method makes use of the inherent textural quality of the paper itself to achieve unique and pleasing results.

MATERIALS
Wood sticks (assorted sizes and kinds)
Paint (powdered or liquid tempera)
Water and paint containers (cans, muffin tins)
Painting surfaces (rice paper, tissue, butcher paper, construction paper, and newspaper)

Making a selection from a variety of sticks.

The stick may be split or carved to prepare it for painting.

Paint should be mixed or poured into containers which have enough depth to allow the sticks to be dipped.

Large color areas are being applied by "scruffing" with paint-laden sticks.

The edges of sticks can be used for fine lines, and smaller sticks used for applying thinner lines. Here details are being applied to the painting.

The finished painting.

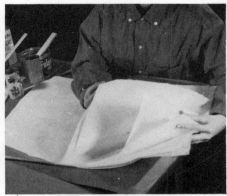

The pupil is shown with several layers of rice paper which may be used in a different approach to stick painting.

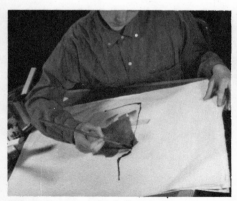

The paint is applied first in larger areas, then developed with lines. Here a chopstick is used to paint lines.

The under layers of rice paper absorb the paint in different degrees. Often one of the papers near the bottom will show the most interesting effects.

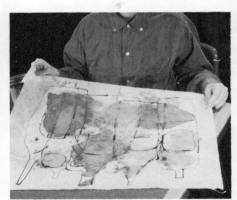

The rice paper with the most pleasing effect is selected and developed further.

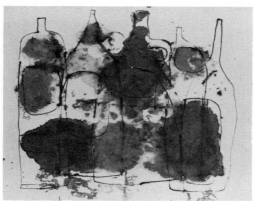

The finished painting.

EXAMPLES OF STICK PAINTING
(See also Frontispiece)

Combined stick and brush painting

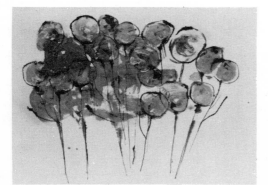

Combined stick and cardboard painting

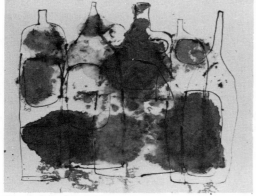

Combined stick and squeegee painting

9. Brush Painting

The brush has been an important painting tool for many centuries. It is possibly as old as civilization itself and it continues to serve as the most popular and useful of all the tools available to the painter.

There are distinct advantages in having brushes of varying sizes and shapes available when the pupil begins to explore with paint. Most well-constructed brushes, if maintained properly, can serve for an indefinite period of time. However, hard, continued usage or improper maintenance can shorten the span of usefulness for any brush. Another advantage of the brush is that a reasonably good one will assure a reliable and somewhat predictable response as the pupil becomes adept in its use. More precise or planned paintings become easier for the pupil to attain. This is not to say that unpredictable or accidental effects do not happen when one becomes proficient in the use of the brush. However, the other methods described in this book make use of painting tools that cannot always be controlled as well.

The brush does have some limitations as a painting tool. Good, well-made brushes are somewhat expensive. To provide a pupil with the many sizes and kinds of brushes that have been designed for specific uses would be a source of considerable expense.

Some brushes are designed to serve a particular task in painting. For instance, the flat, wide brush performs well as a wash or covering tool (for filling in large areas quickly). The smaller, round brushes are usually designed for line design and detail.

If the available supply of brushes is limited, each one must serve many purposes. The pupil should explore the possibilities of each available brush to discover how the various paints and surfaces react to them.

In order to observe, record, and remember these possibilities, it is suggested that the pupil prepare some kind of notebook or exploratory folder as a means of recording preliminary experiments, before proceeding to the actual brush-painting experiences. To do this, he can divide his painting surface into a number of rectangular shapes by folding or scoring it into eight or ten or more separate compartments. In each of these spaces he should try a different approach in using the brush. For instance, in one space he might be asked to apply washes of several colors in rapid succession to see what happens when different colors run together. In the remaining spaces on the sheet the pupil can make other experiments, including wet-on-dry and, possibly, dry brush (a heavier, dryer paint brushed over a previously applied color wash). In some areas, the pupil might drop several colors from the brush into a clear water wash. These suggestions should serve as a springboard to many other experiments of his own so that the pupil begins to feel comfortable with the procedure of preparing color trials. Subsequently, the remaining spaces should be reserved for the pupil's free experiments (his own attempts to discover how brush and color react to each other).

Paintings developed with the brush may be approached in a number of ways. It is often helpful to understand such methods of painting as "dark-to-light" and "light-to-dark." Dark-to-light simply means that the pupil paints all (or most) of his *dark colors first*, then paints his middle-value colors and, finally, his light colors. Light-to-dark is the opposite approach. A painting may be started by painting in the *middle-value colors first*, then painting some light and some dark colors into the remaining areas until the painting is completed. Generally, the pupil has more success starting with large areas of paint (either light or dark) then working into the smaller areas until the very last stage when the final details are painted. This is the most orderly approach to finishing a painting with a brush.

Another way to begin is to paint in the composition with lines using a medium-size brush (½ inch flat or a No. 12 round). Any color may be used for this basic line plan. It should, however, be darker than the painting surface unless, of course, the painting surface is itself dark in color; then a lighter line painting is necessary. With this approach the spaces between the lines are filled in with a somewhat more opaque color. The overlapping of the lines themselves in most instances prevents the work from appearing rigid or overly planned. With further development or the addition of more colors to sections of previously applied paint, allowing the undercolor to peek through will result in a richness of overall color and line and a final result very different from that achieved with the first approaches described above.

Selecting a brush.

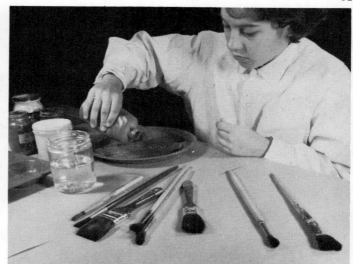

The palette is being filled with paints of different colors. In order to avoid wasting paint, the pupil should determine in advance, as much as possible, colors to be used.

Paintings developed with a brush and using water-soluble paints usually progress in one of two ways. The paintings that show overlapping and clear-color changes to the best advantage are those developed with transparent watercolors (individual color pans in a set or tube colors). These colors are highly pigmented with very little opaque binder so that the finished paintings have somewhat the same characteristics as a stained glass window. Transparent colors that are applied over dried undercolors very frequently do not pick up or lift the undercolor; thus planes or shapes will begin to build up with a definite third color or value resulting from the succeeding washes of transparent color being applied over one another. On the other hand, opaque watercolors (tempera or tempera cakes) have certain binding agents that make the colors heavier with more covering or hiding quality, which does not readily allow undercolor or overlapping color applications to show through in the same manner that transparent colors do. This does not mean that it is not possible for the pupil to achieve undercolor results by using opaque colors. The brush laden with opaque color may be manipulated in such a manner that the undercolor is not entirely covered with additional applications. By this we mean applying the succeeding color layers in a painting sparingly, not allowing complete coverage over previously applied colors. A different kind of color play or sparkle will be observed in a pupil's work when he begins to understand the importance of the undercolor and the over painting and how they are developed differently with each process.

As a supporting tool for other methods of painting, the brush certainly has no peer. In developing variations of other ways of painting described in this book, the pupil should make good use of his brushes. They are standard equipment and should be considered one of the most valuable of painting tools.

MATERIALS

Brushes (flat and round, various sizes)
Palette (trays, dishes, muffin tins)
Paint (tempera, liquid, paste, or powdered; transparent watercolors, pans, tubes)
Water containers (cans, jars, pans)
Painting surfaces (newsprint, newspaper, construction, butcher, drawing, rice, and tissue papers, cardboard, press board, pulp paper)

The pupil wets the brush before mixing colors. A jar filled with clean water is a necessity in brush painting.

Colors are usually mixed on the palette. However, they can sometimes be mixed on the painting surface.

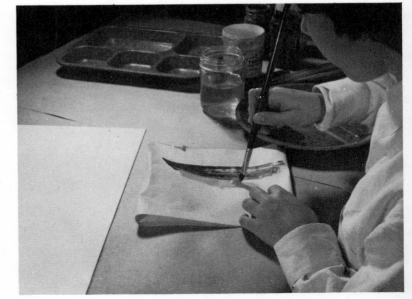

Testing the colors on paper toweling before applying them to the painting surface.

53

The pupil begins the outline of her composition. Sometimes guide lines are used, sometimes not, depending on how the pupil approaches his work.

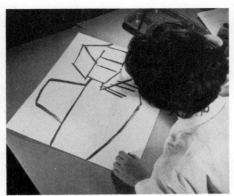

Completing the preliminary structure lines.

Blocks of color are brushed in as the painting develops.

Final details are added with a smaller brush.

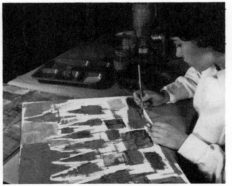

Extra paint can be applied to another painting surface. Some pupils can work on two or more paintings simultaneously.

Brush on pulp paper

Brush and cardboard combination

Brush and spatula combination

EXAMPLES OF BRUSH PAINTING

Experiments with the brush

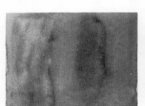

flat tone

wet-in-wet

graduated wash

splatter

2-color graduated wash

strokes

dry brush

experimental

Basic Elements of Composition

Possibly the simplest definition of composition is *the arrangement of the painting's lines, planes, masses, and surface quality*. In discussing composition with pupils, there is no one formula that will solve all problems. However, it may be helpful to settle on a simple vocabulary that will be reasonably easy to understand. Explanations should be provided that do not prove overly-complicated, technical, or dull.

With this in mind, we shall proceed to discuss the four main structural elements to consider when we try to help pupils understand and improve their own works. Some highly technical treatments of this subject will cover as many as six or eight major elements, but for the purpose of this book, a less complex approach is desirable.

The four basic elements, *line, plane, mass,* and *surface quality,* have simple definitions that will soon make the pupil aware of the importance of each to the whole painting process.

Line. Line may establish boundaries, define contours, and form patterns. It is also a means of giving a detailed quality to a painting. It may sharpen the appearance of any given area of the work and assist the eye in moving from one area of the painting to another by serving as a network. An example is the stained glass window, which separates colors by the use of line.

Plane. The flat shapes in a painting that have no visual thickness may be thought of as planes. These shapes have width and also length but no depth. Planes allow the pupil a means of variety through combination with lines or one of the other elements to create contrast in a composition. Examples are the planes of buildings, trees, or figures contrasted against flat sky.

Mass. The solid appearing elements of a painting are called mass. They lend a feeling of thickness or volume to parts of the painting. This three-dimensional appearance can also be thought of as "form." An example is a hollow or solid object that shows form by light-dark value relationships (shading), by changes of color (warm to cool), or differences in texture.

Surface Quality. This element includes both *color* and *texture.* Color in a painting gives either brilliance or dullness, depending upon the combination of various colors and their values. Texture is the development of a rough-to-smooth or light-to-dark surface quality. It may be produced in a variety of ways. An example of surface quality using both color and texture is demonstrated when a pupil applies paint over a previously painted area but allows the undercolor to show through to form a surface pattern.

Teachers should look at a pupil's painting with the following questions in mind: How well has each of the four elements been used? Does the painting need more line development to hold it together? Does the surface of a particular area of the work seem too flat and, therefore, uninteresting? Would texture improve this part of the painting? Should an area of interest be emphasized more? Which element would serve best to do this? As soon as the pupil is able to understand, with simple and not overly-technical explanations, what these elements will do, he will begin to ask these questions of himself without further teacher stimulation.

These four structural elements and their importance should be reemphasized from time to time. However, they also should be approached in different ways and expanded upon at different levels of the pupil's maturity. For example, if a young pupil paints continually at the bottom of the paper or to one side or has difficulty in completing certain areas, the teacher might encourage him to relocate or rearrange the structure of his painting, by helping him to understand the need for a balance of the elements. In other words, an "overweighting" of his composition in one direction or another might be explained to him as a "falling down" in the painting surface of his subject matter. This is not to suggest that all paintings must have equal or formal balance, but by the use of simple descriptive statements one might be able to encourage the pupil to see why some paintings hold together and have balance while other paintings appear not to.

Balance can be either *formal* or *dynamic* (informal). Formal balance is accomplished by the use of symmetry. Dynamic balance can be achieved in many ways, such as balancing a large, light-colored element in one part of the painting by a small, dark-colored element in an opposite area. There are innumerable ways of creating balance in painting, but this should not be a source of worry to the teacher because balance may be achieved intuitively as well as intellectually. In other words, one does not need to justify balance scientifically in a painting. The painting may simply "look" or "feel" balanced or achieve a movement by being slightly "out" of balance. At the earlier levels of painting, it is doubly important that discussions of composition not be *overly* technical. Each illustration or explanation should be given to the pupil through several different, easily-understood approaches. The terms, as such, should not be memorized to the exclusion of the meanings themselves. There will be ample time for the technical approach as the pupil reaches real maturity in painting.

One of the natural questions that teachers frequently ask is "Is it advisable for a pupil to make a drawing first before beginning a painting, or should he begin to work directly on the painting surface with only guide lines or a sketch?" It might be agreed that painting directly onto the surface without the use of a drawing usually insures greater spontaneity or freshness in the work. However, it might also be said that some pupils may gain confidence and find it of value to make preliminary small sketches or notes while jotting down their impressions of what they are planning as a possible painting experiment. These brief idea sketches may be recorded on a pad or scrap paper for future use. For many pupils this will constitute a valuable form of research, much like that which is encouraged in any discipline as a means of retaining valuable information for use at a later time.

One other purpose of stressing good composition is the challenge it gives the pupil to fill the paper with well-thought-out shapes, forms, and colors rather than to leave white or blank areas which have little relationship to the total painting. Sometimes the pupil may not be aware that he is leaving parts of his painting unattended or unfinished. It is interesting and quite revealing for the pupil to turn his painting upside down, look for possible faults, and then discuss the problems of composition and color distribution with the teacher. By observing his painting upside down or sideways, the pupil may discover, without being unduly influenced by subject matter, how effectively the elements of composition are being developed. This and further methods of careful study by the pupil of his work and that of others will reveal to him the many possible smaller subdivisions in his paintings. He will soon become used to laying down large shapes of color first to insure a good start. Then he will work back over his painting, breaking these larger areas into a variety of textures and/or smaller shapes. Finally, he will begin to develop that important interplay of *depths* in his paintings that is so often missing in many beginner's work.

The study of composition is probably the least emphasized and the least understood of the many facets of painting. Pupils do seem to go right on painting regardless of whether or not any direction in this area is given to them. However, it is most important for the pupil to be at least exposed to the structural elements that play such an important role in painting. As with anything else, an overemphasis or continual technical reference to composition can be dull, especially for the very young pupil. The study of composition and its elements should always be presented in combination with the study of painting and should be presented in a manner that is understandable at the pupil's particular level of development.

Students should be exposed to inspirational examples of good composition. These include reproductions of master paintings; photographs or actual examples of structural design elements that may be related to painting, such as *textures* in fabrics, wood or bark; and *lines* found in trees, houses, and boats. If pupils are encouraged to look for these elements, they will discover them in all well-designed things.

Fundamentals of Color

In this book, the approach to color emphasizes ways for the pupil to work directly with color rather than deal with its technical or theoretical aspects. It is adequate (and preferable) to use the simplest of terms.

However, some background in color theory is very helpful to all pupils, especially when the presentation is short, to the point, and embellished with interesting props or visual aids. Such a presentation should deal first with an introduction to the *primary* colors—*red, yellow,* and *blue.* The *secondary* colors should then be shown—*orange, green,* and *violet.* Finally, it could be demonstrated how these colors combine to form other intermediate hues—*yellow-orange, blue-violet, red-orange, blue-green,* and *red-violet.* All of the above colors comprise the well-known color wheel. The accompanying brief sketches indicate how visual aids for these color theories could be prepared by the teacher or, if desired, by pupils.

The three basic properties of color are *hue, value,* and *intensity* (see Glossary). While value is the most difficult for the pupil to understand, it is often the key to successful color use. A simple value scale is, therefore, an important aid to the understanding of color. It is usually made with only one color or black. The first step is to lay out, as a guide, a series of squares with pencil on paper. The single color or black is then applied to these squares in a sequence of shades from the darkest value of the color in the first square to the lightest value in the last square. The value scale which usually suits the purpose best is the five-value chart shown here: (1) Dark (2) Medium-dark (3) Medium (4)

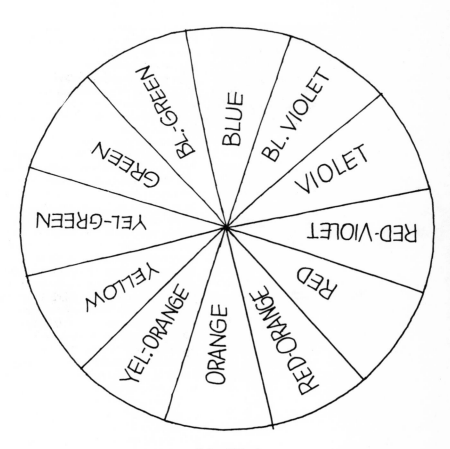

Color Wheel

Value Scale

Dark

Medium-dark

Medium

Medium-light

Light

Medium-light, and (5) Light. To achieve lighter values, more water, or white, is mixed with the paint. To achieve darker values, less water or more black is used.

In addition to learning to mix colors from the observation of their natural appearance in the world around them, pupils should be encouraged to develop an intuitive approach to color. Colors have strong emotional and psychological meanings for all of us. Red calls to mind fire and heat, blue projects feelings of coolness and self-containment. We associate green with spring and growing things. Purple and black can create moods rich with mystery. Pupils should not be discouraged from using color combinations that have particular meanings for them, even if they depart from what we traditionally hold to be visual "truth." For example, a sky can be successfully painted almost any color, and so can flowers and even animals and people—as a study of the works of great painters throughout history will show. Suggestions from the teacher regarding the use of colors should be carefully considered. The age-old inhibitions on the use of certain "unfit" color combinations (such as the "vibrating" colors opposite on the color wheel) should be ignored. Almost any combination of colors can produce exciting results. Setting up too many restrictions is not conducive to maximum creative development.

Color used straight from the jar is often unsatisfactory because of its "rawness." Pupils should be encouraged to experiment in mixing colors together in many combinations to produce greater vitality and subtlety. Colors can be lightened by adding white paint or water and darkened by adding black or other dark colors. Color brilliance or intensity is sometimes sacrificed to some extent when mixing colors in this way.

Using a limited palette of one, two, or three colors is often a rewarding experience. Many times a pleasing unity of color is achieved in this way. An effective method of exploring with only a few colors is to limit the color choices to either warm colors or cool colors. The warm palette may include yellows, oranges or reds. The cool palette might include hues of green and blue. Black and white may be added to these limited palettes to allow the pupil to gray some of his colors.

There are several ways for the pupil to mix and blend colors: (1) He may mix colors on the palette before applying them to his painting; (2) he may mix the colors on the painting surface itself during application; or (3) he may apply fresh color *over* previously dried color on the painting and thereby achieve a mixture or a change in hue.

Since paint often dries lighter than it appears when applied in a wet state, it may be advisable to encourage pupils to use strong or bright colors (not necessarily "raw") in order to retain color strength in their finished paintings and to avoid a weak or washed-out effect.

Since many pupils' paintings contain large flat color areas, some of which may be lacking in interest, there should be an effort made to demonstrate how these flat areas can be made more interesting. *Textural* quality can be added to such areas by applying paint with a thick consistency and allowing variations of the thickness to achieve the desired surface quality.

Working with color can be very enjoyable when the pupil experiments to see what happens as he mixes, applies, and changes colors. This knowledge can offer the pupil many opportunities for success. Even the experiments which turn into disappointments are valuable. Accomplished painters use such experiences as a learning process while discovering further pleasures of exploring with paint.

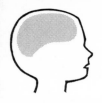

Setting the Mood

There seems to be a direct relation between a pupil's enthusiasm to explore in painting and the environment provided for this exploration. The responsibility for establishing the desired atmosphere must rest with the teacher. Only he is familiar with all the factors involved, such as the nature of the pupils themselves, the available facilities, and the limitations of time and expense.

The atmosphere that offers the most encouragement and favorable stimulus for the pupil need not be the result of new or spacious surroundings or expensive equipment and supplies. Almost any surrounding can be made visually, mentally, and emotionally stimulating and, thereby, arouse some feeling of excitement for creative expression. As part of a necessary understanding of mood setting, there must be the realization that pupils will gain skill and confidence in painting if they become aware at the outset that they will experience both enjoyment and frustration in painting experiences. Total success is seldom achieved in any endeavor, and painting is certainly no exception. A high degree of success is possible, however, if a realistic attitude is adopted. While it is important to maintain a healthy, happy, and optimistic attitude, a too lighthearted, "fun-and-games" approach may ultimately lead to more frustrations than successes. With this in mind, the following major areas of concern in motivating pupils to explore with paint are important:

Physical Setting of the Classroom

Many classrooms, not serving exclusively as art rooms, have precious little display space to spare for inspirational materials. Teachers can open up a wide range of ideas for the pupil through the use of movable displays. This should be con-sidered a *group* motivation process. (Individual motivation, which will be discussed later, is a different matter.)

A very effective group-motivation technique is to establish a small inspiration corner within the classroom for display purposes. A bulletin board should be set up (if one is not already there) on which to display visual materials, such as reproductions of all kinds from periodicals and newspapers, reproductions of contemporary and old masters' paintings and drawings, photographs, art from ancient civilizations, and art pertaining to the local region. Magazines and art books offer much inspiration for pupils. By using some ingenuity, these resource materials can be strategically displayed in the classroom instead of, as sometimes happens, buried in a crowded bookcase with only edges or backs showing. A well-thought-out display should be inviting to look at, or to pick up and study, and a strong source of motivation.

When displaying visual materials, the teacher should exercise some caution to prevent them from becoming a handy source for direct copying. By changing the displays frequently, this problem can be minimized and pupils will use the visual material as a springboard in developing ideas of their own.

The use of interesting color schemes and textures in the room can also help provide a favorable background for painting. Drab classrooms tend to be depressing to teachers and pupils alike. The bulk of the work connected with establishing this interior embellishment need not always be assumed by the teacher. Pupils can help in collecting, storing, and displaying materials, particularly the older and more interested ones. Displays and set-ups should be changed rather frequently or at least before interest in them has faded—a three-week limit for any one display is a reasonable recommendation.

A Good Beginning For the Painting Session

Some pupils are consistently successful in starting a painting, while others may frequently be at a loss for ideas. This inconsistency of mood is also characteristic of many professional artists who may find themselves in a "dry spell" during which they find it difficult to work up fresh ideas. Unfortunately, it is impossible to turn creative imagination on and off like a light switch. However, the teacher may be somewhat pleasantly surprised to learn that shaping the mood of a class by establishing an atmosphere conducive to creative expression is not as difficult as one might imagine.

In starting a painting session, it is the teacher's responsibility to encourage the pupil's enthusiasm for exploration. It is strongly suggested that the teacher first explore the process alone and then demonstrate it to the class before the pupils undertake the procedure individually. This procedure has several advantages. The teacher, in becoming familiar with the process, will probably become more enthusiastic about it, will be better able to anticipate its difficulties and pitfalls, and will also be able to understand the limitations as well as the materials needed.

It is also a good idea for the teacher to become actively and enthusiastically involved in each painting session, preferably by exploring along with the pupils. This does a great deal to develop confidence in the pupil and to impress him with the discovery that his painting activity is a worthwhile endeavor enjoyed by adults also. Some caution should be taken, however, to see that pupils do not attempt to repeat only what the teacher is doing.

In regard to the problems of getting

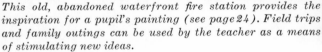
This old, abandoned waterfront fire station provides the inspiration for a pupil's painting (see page 24). Field trips and family outings can be used by the teacher as a means of stimulating new ideas.

ideas at the beginning of a painting session, one is reminded of Beethoven's statement, "You will ask me where I get my ideas . . . . they come unsummoned . . . . in the open air . . . . in the woods . . . . at dawn . . . ." Some pupils will have an abundance of ideas for painting, perhaps all different, while others will tend to concentrate on one theme or idea and proceed to develop variations of it in their work. Both approaches have merit, but variations of each should be encouraged so that the painting sessions do not become boring. There are many ways to start a painting successfully. Some pupils strive for moods in their paintings, giving little attention to specific detail. Others are more comfortable in composing their work by using details right at the start as a means of creating a "structure" upon which to build. Teachers should be aware of the different approaches to painting so that pupils do not get the impression that there is only *one* way to express their ideas.

What to paint can become a delicate concern. Pupils may or may not need specific visual stimulation. Many times it is mutually inspiring for the teacher to point out and discuss with the pupil the wonders of the world that surround him. This technique can be achieved through verbal reminiscing of first-hand experience such as field trips, family excursions, and vicarious experiences with photographs or other visual-aid materials. The pupil can be encouraged to observe, remember, and share verbally his thoughts about such stimulating topics as birds and animals, unusual patterns emerging in a scrap heap, the facades of building, and open sections in docks, streets, and skylines. Pupils can develop these impressions as alternatives to, or parts of, the familiar sky, sun, and sea that appear in so many of their paintings. They may become inspired merely by being reminded of interesting places they have visited or by being asked about places they would like to visit. Feelings about music or poetry can serve as another idea source. Sometimes an extra painting surface near the painting being worked on can be used to apply leftover color on, in an intuitive manner, with no specific plan or idea in mind at the time. This extra painting may take on interest as the colors are applied in this casual manner. In fact, many excellent paintings can be produced in this way. The "second" painting with the left-over color often has an informal, fresh, and spontaneous appearance not found in the first.

Mood setting and motivation can very often be the key to continued enthusiasm.

Inspirational, thought-provoking displays stressing good composition help to establish an atmosphere that encourages exploratory painting.

Publications devoted to art can be attractively displayed to invite examination.

It is important that the teacher explore the various painting processes first. Here the teacher experiments with the collage process, using colored tissue and a transparent glue. By experimenting before offering the process to the pupils, the teacher may avoid most unforseen problems.

Evaluating Paintings

Providing a pupil with a critical analysis of his painting, while attempting at the same time to encourage him to explore freely (often with ample opportunities for failure), presents a real problem for teachers. It is easy to become either overly lenient or too strict in evaluating if care is not taken to prevent this from happening.

For many teachers, it is a far more difficult task to attempt to evaluate a pupil's creative efforts than to evaluate his other more measurable areas of learning. In some cases, evaluation of paintings has deteriorated to such vague, unexplained critical judgments as "S" for satisfactory or "U" for unsatisfactory. Such an evaluation is of little more value than no evaluation at all. Pupils who receive such an analysis of their work cannot help but assume that their efforts were not worthy or that the instructor is not capable of an honest evaluation.

At the other extreme are the over-evaluated pupils who are constantly being interrupted or stopped short in their experimentation to have their work analyzed, discussed, and graded.

Either of these extreme situations is harmful to the pupils' morale and to the maintenance of their enthusiasm. To prevent delay in the pupils' orderly growth in painting, a middle ground in the evaluation process needs to be established by the teacher. Critical analysis of each pupil's work should be made, but on a reasonable basis. A pupil needs time to work freely as well as time to think carefully about his progress in painting. Several methods of evaluation are outlined below to show opportunities and approaches that have proven successful in the classroom.

One method of critical analysis is the group-discussion approach. If paintings of four or five pupils can be discussed at one time, then it is suggested that some different and particularly effective area of each pupil's work be pointed out and discussed with the whole group. For example, one pupil's painting may have as its best feature harmony of color. Another may have an interesting use of texture, or excellent composition. Thus, each of the paintings being evaluated by the student group may be considered successful by at least one standard. Each pupil's work represented in these group discussions can become a source of real inspiration and critical thinking for the individual as well as for all other pupils. Furthermore, to have his painting discussed by others is, in itself, recognition of a pupil's efforts. It is a definite means of stimulating further exploration and study. Another advantage of the group-discussion method is that the pupil is encouraged to talk about his own work and to ask questions concerning the work of others. This searching "question and answer" period stimulates the pupils' interest in painting and is most important for further growth.

Pupils need, also, to have individual evaluation of their work from time to time. To provide it in a valid way, the teacher should develop an approach that is logical and understandable to the pupil. These standards should be simple and direct, particularly on the beginning levels. More complex criteria can be reserved for the advanced levels of painting.

In this book three main criteria are considered for evaluating paintings on an individual basis. When judged by these standards, each pupil's work should be considered with his own growth and potential in mind—where he started and where he is now, *not* in terms of how his work ranks in relation to others in a given group.

1. *Imagination:* How successfully does the pupil express and incorporate his own ideas into his paintings without continual teacher stimulation or other technical assistance?
2. *Composition:* How successfully does the pupil combine his paintings' structural elements—*color, mass, shape,* and *line*—into a harmonious work?
3. *Use of Tools and Materials:* How skillfully does the pupil adapt the available tools and materials to express his ideas?

As mentioned earlier, when evaluating a pupil's painting, it is strongly recommended that it be analyzed by comparison with his past work. This method of allowing the pupil to "compete against himself" usually works much better than comparing one pupil's work with others in the class. By using this system, it is more likely that the superior pupil will not grow complacent, and the less capable pupil will not lose enthusiasm.

In order to check the progress of his work, each pupil should construct a large manila folder, no smaller than 19 x 13 inches for inside measurements. The folder can be used to store examples of his work. Thus he may judge his own progress over a period of time. Each work may be dated when it is placed in the folder.

As mentioned previously, it is important to individual growth for the teacher to select from each pupil's work its most effective aspect. A notation on the back of each work commenting on the sensitive use of color, interesting composition, imaginative use of texture, or anything well done will be of encouragement. Each pupil has a potential for effective creative expression in some facet of painting, and it should be the concern of the teacher to try to help each one gain confidence through any special assets possessed. A highly successful effort in any one of the three criteria might well make a given work creditable. There are paintings that, by professional standards, have been considered successful with less than the three criteria being served. For instance, a painting may have some merit from a design and composition standpoint even though a poor use of material has been made. To say that each criterion is comparable to one-third of the evaluation of a pupil's work would not be entirely reasonable. It is the intent to offer these three criteria as a general guide for the evaluation of paintings. Each individual effort should be evaluated not in a rigid sense, but with a flexible use of the three criteria. The resulting evaluation will generate enthusiasm in the pupil and encourage him to cope with and try to solve further problems in his creative growth.

It should again be emphasized that *self-evaluation* by the pupil, what he himself likes best about his work, or what he feels is least successful about his own efforts, will do much to encourage him to become constructively critical. This is true at all age levels.

Each pupil should have an opportunity for individual evaluation of his work. Close personal discussion of the work with the teacher can help stimulate further exploration.

If the pupils' paintings are dated upon completion (with rubber stamp dater as shown) a record of comparing past efforts with present progress can be kept.

Exhibiting Paintings

Exhibiting pupils' work is more important than many realize. The painting session itself is usually not enough to satisfy entirely the needs of most pupils, even though inner satisfaction is sometimes all that a pupil will need from his work. A painting is a mental and emotional experience to be studied and enjoyed not only by its creator but by others as well. This is also true of poetry, the dance, drama, and music. Usually there is a felt need for audience recognition of any creative effort; the artist wants to know that what he has done is meaningful to others. Exhibition of his efforts, therefore, is a vital part of the total painting experience.

Choice of Display Paintings

There are two common methods used in the selection of paintings for exhibition. The first is to exhibit the work of all pupils at the same time. The main drawback to this approach is that the lack of exhibition space in most classrooms prevents a really attractive display of this kind. If facilities are available for an exhibit that is well designed and does not appear overcrowded, this universal representation is preferred. The second method is to exhibit only a few paintings at a time with a schedule for rotating the display so that eventually everyone will have a work shown.

Several methods may be successfully used to group the paintings for exhibition. Groups may be arranged alphabetically. However, another approach is to display groups of paintings on the basis of some common ground, such as similarity in subject matter or color scheme. Once the paintings are classified into groups, the exhibition schedule is determined so that eventually all paintings are exhibited. This procedure is valuable because it can serve as an instructional aid stressing particular qualities learned in the painting sessions.

Display Facilities

The best area for exhibiting paintings is the classroom. However, there are other strategic locations in most school buildings, such as hallways and the library, which should be used as much as possible so that all can share in the art program.

An excellent method of providing portable exhibits of paintings on a large scale is to use simple "A"-frame display easels. These easels are constructed with a pegboard surface on two sides and with hinged, folding legs on both ends to allow for ease of storage when not in use. If the easels are to be used out of doors, galvanized screening or chicken wire may be substituted for the pegboard. This type of display easel is particularly effective because it provides a means of exhibiting paintings in areas that do not have suitable wall hanging space or corkboard wall panels.

Matting Paintings

Paintings are most effectively displayed when they are matted. The simplest mat is a cardboard or paper frame which fits around the painting and sets it off in a pleasing manner. Mats should be white, gray, or natural in color; an elaborate or colorful mat tends to detract from the painting. Oversize and undersize mats can also detract attention.

A pleasing proportion for a mat is three inches at the top and sides, and three and one half inches at the bottom. The cut-out area of the mat should measure at least one half inch smaller on all four sides than the painting itself. After the dimensions of the mat have been penciled on the mat material, it is cut out with a mat knife or razor blade and a straightedge. Masking tape is used to tape the edges of the painting firmly to the backside of the mat.

Mounting Paintings

Another way to set off a painting is to mount it on top of a heavier cardboard, larger than the finished painting, thus providing a "framed" effect similar to the

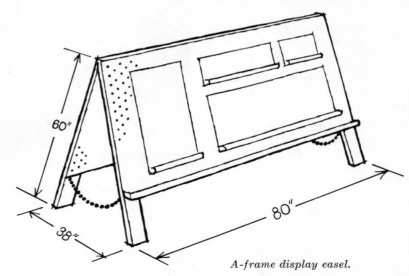

A-frame display easel.

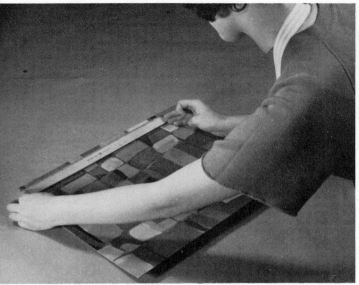

Measuring the painting for a mat.

After transferring the measurements of the painting to the mat board, the student rules the guidelines for cutting the opening.

The size of the opening should allow for at least a ½-inch overlap on all four sides of the painting.

Removing the inside cutout from the mat. This rectangle can later be used as a smaller mat or as an extra painting surface.

By attaching small masking tape tabs to the four sides of the painting, it can be positioned inside the mat.

By laying the mat over the painting the pupil makes use of positioning tabs to insure accurate contact.

To insure a clean appearance, strips of tape are applied on all four sides of the painting. This additional taping helps reduce gaps between painting and mat.

Setting up an exhibit.

Attractive, light, free-standing display panels may be used effectively where display cases are not available. These units bolt together and are easily dismantled and moved.

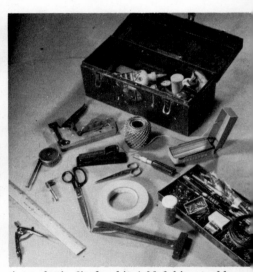

A teacher's display kit (old fishing tackle box) contains many useful display tools and materials, including a single-point stapler, an adjustable rule, and assorted tacks, string, and pins.

mat technique. The same margin proportions, three inches for the top and sides the three-and-a-half inches at the bottom, may also be used when mounting paintings.

The materials used for matting and mounting may vary from thin and fragile paper, such as construction or drawing paper, to heavy matboard, such as illustration board or pebble-surface matboard. As a general rule, the heavier boards make better mats, but they are more expensive.

Mats and mounts serve the valuable purpose of separating paintings from cluttered or distracting backgrounds and focusing attention on the work itself. A simple gray or subdued background area in a display space may eliminate the need for matting and mounting. This is particularly true when the paintings are strong enough in color and composition to stand apart from the display background.

Teachers often find it helpful to fashion some kind of display kit for their own use in the classroom. A good container can be made from a fishing tackle box. The tools need not be expensive or of great variety.

With the assortment shown it is an easy matter to create new exhibits.

By exhibiting pupils' paintings in the school, and in the community, the teacher provides a climate to stimulate and inspire all who view these works and, at the same time, offers real encouragement to the young painters themselves.

Glossary of Painting Terms

Advancing Colors—Warm colors which seem to assert themselves and, therefore, move to the front in a painting.

Aesthetics—The philosophy of beauty.

Analogous Colors—Colors near each other on the color wheel.

Associative Colors—Colors which may evoke thoughts, images, or concepts.

Balance—An arrangement of elements which achieves equilibrium in the eye of the viewer; can be formal balance or dynamic balance.

Binder—The material (such as gum arabic) which binds pigment particles in paint.

Bleeding—Under-painting color seeping through overpainting color, or color spreading into an adjacent color.

Body—The covering power or strength of a pigment.

Body Color—Colors mixed with white or other colors to make them more opaque.

Broken Color—Color areas "broken up" by the addition of other colors.

Casein-base Glue—A glue useful in making collage paintings; it is transparent when dry.

Casein Paint—A water-soluble, opaque paint with a dairy-product base.

Chroma—Intensity or brightness of a color.

Clashing Colors—Colors which do not appear to go together, either because of prejudice or because they do not harmonize in a pleasing manner; sometimes called vibrating colors.

Color Balance—A pleasing arrangement of colors forming an apparent "balance" of hue, value, and intensity.

Color Scheme—The plan or arrangement of colors within a painting.

Content—The visual meaning of a painting.

Contrast—In painting, the differences or comparisons apparent among the elements.

Cool Colors—Blues, greens, and their variants.

Counter Change—Dark-against-light and light-against-dark used alternately in the same painting.

Density—Color opaqueness.

Design—Basic plan or organization in a painting.

Distortion—Deliberate departure from the normal appearance of an object or figure for an aesthetic purpose.

Dominance—Relative importance of elements in a painting.

Dry Brush—Technique of painting with a brush in a relatively "dry" state, containing only a small amount of paint to produce a unique textural quality.

Eye Level—The horizon line as used in perspective.

Gouache—Another name for opaque watercolor.

Graduated Color—Color which blends gradually from one value, chroma, or hue into another.

Ground—Painting surface.

Harmony—In painting, a combination of elements which achieves a pleasing, orderly whole.

Hue—Color.

Impasto—Thick, paste-like paint.

Juxtaposition—The placement of colors side by side or close together.

Light and Shade—Graduated values of colors used in a painting to distinguish between contour, dimension, or volume.

Limited Palette—A restricted selection of colors used to offer an additional challenge for pupils by increasing their awareness of dark and light.

Local Color—The true color of an object as seen by the eye and uninfluenced by surrounding colors.

Mat Surface—A dull, nonreflecting surface.

Medium—1. The material used (paint, wood, etc.). 2. The fluid added to paint to alter its consistency.

Modeling—Defining forms, achieving an illusion of depth or volume in drawing and painting.

Motif—Theme.

Movement—An element of composition that "leads" or "moves" the eye in the desired direction.

Negative Space—The space between lines or forms, considered important as rests or stops; the opposite of the positive shapes or lines.

Open Form—A type of composition which allows space to penetrate its masses.

Pigment—The powdered coloring agent of paint.

Powdered Clay—Clay in powder form added as a thickening agent to water-soluble paints.

Proportion—The relationship in size of one part of a painting to other parts within it as well as to the totality of all the parts.

Raw Colors—Colors as they are manufactured, unmixed with other colors.

Reflected Color—Color that is reflected onto an area from another source.

Repetition—The repeating of elements within a painting.

Retreating Colors—Colors that suggest distance, such as the cool colors.

Rhythm—Pattern of flow or movement in a painting.

Secondary Colors—Green, orange, and violet.

Subordination—Playing down elements in a painting which are of the least importance.

Symbolic Color—Color that stands for or represents a specific thought or emotion.

Symmetry—Bilateral arrangement of forms creating an equalized division of areas in a painting.

Tactile Quality—Textural surface quality of a painting.

Tempera—A water-soluble paint which dries with a non-glossy finish.

Tertiary Colors—Colors formed by mixing a primary and a secondary color: blue-violet, blue-green, yellow-green, yellow-orange, red-orange, red-violet.

Tint—Gradation of color by mixing with white.

Tonality—Relative degree to which white or dark has been added to a color, thereby changing its intensity.

Tone—Combined effect of light, shade, and color in a painting.

Transferring—Sometimes used to describe the process of transferring a drawing from paper to a painting surface by first applying pencil carbon to the back of the drawing and then pressing the image onto the painting surface by redrawing each line.

Triad—Three related colors (e.g., red, yellow, blue).

Underpainting—The first application of paint to a painting onto which subsequent layers are added.

Value—The dark-to-light relationship of tones, tints, or colors according to the amount of light reflected from the painting surface.

Vibrating Colors—Two complementary colors of equal intensity juxtaposed.

Warm Colors—Reds, yellows, and oranges and their admixtures.

Wash—A thinned, watery coat of paint.

Wet-into-wet—Technique of watercolor painting in which paint is applied onto a wet surface or two wet colors are used in combination, thus achieving blending within the painting.